A PLACE TO HIDE

ROGER F. CAMPBELL

While this book is designed for the reader's personal enjoyment and profit, it is also intended for group study. A Leader's Guide with Victor Multiuse Transparency Masters is available from your local bookstore or from the publisher.

VICTOR BOOKS a division of SP Publications, Inc.
WHEATON, ILLINOIS 60187

Offices also in
Whitby, Ontario, Canada
Amersham-on-the-Hill, Bucks, England

To receive the author's cassette, "The Revival We Need," send $6.00 to: Roger F. Campbell, P. O. Box 444, Waterford, Michigan 48095.

The Scripture quotations in this book are from the *King James Version.*

Recommended Dewey Decimal Classification: 291.44
  Suggested Subject Headings: CHRISTIAN RENEWAL, SURVIVALISM.

Library of Congress Catalog Card Number: 82-61037
ISBN: 0-88207-383-4

Contents

To my daughters,
Cheryl and Charlene,
women of faith

Preface

The world is in crisis; the church, at a crossroads.

Impatient people, many of them Christian leaders, are tempted to take matters into their own hands in an effort to straighten out the crooked places in our distraught civilization. Others have written off the future of the present social order and are preparing to exit when the sky falls.

A Place to Hide addresses three options currently being promoted as answers to the problems of this difficult period: survivalism, Christian political action, and nuclear brinksmanship. I have attempted to face these proposed routes to survival in the light of history and the teaching of the Scriptures. This book presents not only investigations of these movements, but also a positive plan for a return to the basic Christian principles which carried the first-century church through unspeakable persecution and saw it emerge triumphant. It is a call for a genuine spiritual awakening. Our times are not the first in which men and women have come to the end of themselves and attempted to forsake old ways in the hope of finding a quick fix for problems. In some difficult periods, believers have cried out to God for revival and have been rescued and refreshed from above. As you read about the great revivals of the past, you may find yourself praying along with me, "Lord, do it again!"

He can.

And He will . . . if we meet the conditions.

Roger F. Campbell

1 LIVING ON THE BRINK

Shortly after the birth of the nuclear age, Dr. David Bradley, radiological monitor of early atomic bomb testing, wrote: "When one considers that one-millionth of a gram of radium contained within the body may be fatal, one is inclined to turn from calculus to Christianity" (*No Place to Hide*, Little, Brown, p. 88).

In the early 1960s, the late President John F. Kennedy, sensing the growing menace of nuclear firepower in the world, warned in a State of the Union message that each day drew us nearer to the hour of maximum danger. It is unlikely that even he envisioned today's frightening situation.

We sleep and wake and go about our daily tasks within the missile sights of a powerful enemy bent on our destruction. Our existence is threatened by the whims of fanatic and greedy political leaders, some of whom are the heads of nations that once were considered no threat but which now possess weapons that could plunge the world into a nuclear holocaust.

The Bible speaks of an era of universal danger: "This

11

know also, that in the last days perilous times shall come" (2 Tim. 3:1). Many students of Bible prophecy believe current world developments prove we are living in the countdown to the end. Some secular experts agree:

The editors of the *Bulletin of Atomic Scientists* have developed a "doomsday clock" that measures human history in terms of a 24-hour day. At the end of 1980 the hands of the clock were moved to 4 minutes till midnight because of the escalating nuclear arms race.

In his article, "On the Eve of Destruction," (*Detroit* magazine, Jan. 3, 1982, p. 8), Michael Betzold pointed out three major causes for concern about the likelihood of a nuclear war. One is the proliferation of nuclear weapons in the Soviet and American arsenals. A second is the increasing number of nations and groups now possessing nuclear weapons. The third is a switch in superpower strategy that has changed nuclear war from an inconceivable measure to an increasingly thinkable option.

Today the 6 major nuclear nations have a mind-boggling arsenal of destruction equivalent to 5 tons of TNT for every person on earth. Within a few years as many as 30 other nations may have their own nuclear capabilities. Size then may mean little or nothing when considering a nation's potential for war. This buildup of deadly weapons fits Joel's prophecy that calls for even the weak to say, "I am strong." Joel said, "Proclaim ye this among the Gentiles: Prepare war, wake up the mighty men, let all the men of war draw near, let them come up. Beat your plowshares into swords, and your pruninghooks into spears. Let the weak say, 'I am strong' " (3:9-10).

Can it be that the current huge and increasing world arms cache is a stockpile of war material that is destined for use in the final world conflict? Many think so.

While we do not know how close we may be to that

prophesied holocaust, we know that wars will continue and that they will increase in severity and frequency as the end approaches. Jesus talked about what can be expected.

And ye shall hear of wars and rumors of wars: see that ye be not troubled, . . . for nation shall rise against nation and kingdom against kingdom: and there shall be famines, and pestilences, and earthquakes, in diverse places. . . . For then shall be great tribulation, such as was not since the beginning of the world to this time, now, nor ever shall be. And except those days should be shortened, there should be no flesh saved. But for the elect's sake those days shall be shortened (Matt. 24:6-7, 21-22).

The Apostle Paul compared the signs of the end to the experience of a woman in labor and about to give birth: "For we know that the whole creation groaneth and travaileth in pain together until now. And not only they, but ourselves also, which have the firstfruits of the Spirit, even we ourselves groan within ourselves, waiting for the adoption, to wit, the redemption of our body" (Rom. 8:22-23).

We should not be surprised, then, to find the world in an ever-deepening crisis. International tensions, trouble spots, and natural disasters are but universal labor pains. The earth is in travail. Birth is approaching.

Trouble Spots
The Middle East. The Middle East has become a powder keg. Israel and her neighbors vie for control of areas in that part of the world. Jerusalem is a particular area of contention between Arabs and Jews, bringing Zechariah's prophecy to mind: "Behold, I will make Jerusalem a cup of trembling unto all the people round about, when they shall be in the seige both against Judah and against Jerusalem. And in that day will I make Jerusalem a burdensome stone for all people: All that burden themselves with it shall be cut in pieces,

though all the people of the earth be gathered together against it" (Zech. 12:2-3).

Many Americans look nervously toward the ancient city of Jerusalem and tremble with thoughts of global war. Tough talk by Jews and Arabs about the control of that coveted city only adds to the worries of the world.

Most of us know we are dependent on Middle East countries for vast amounts of energy to operate our factories, to produce our abundant harvests, and even to heat our homes. Periodic long lines at gas stations and inflation, fueled by high energy costs remind us that a lifeline of oil connects us to that dangerous region. Some people fear a wave of anti-Semitism if irritated Americans blame the Jews for recurrent shortages brought on by our support of Israel. Some fear retaliatory measures taken against us by oil-producing Arab nations.

The Soviet Union. And there is the Soviet Union, an eye on the Middle East, edging ever closer to those vital oil fields. Russia, the military giant of this decade. Even Communist China, with its vast reservoir of manpower for military service, cooperates with the West for fear of mighty Russia.

Military experts have long been making frightening statements about the expansionist aims of the Soviet Union, and with Russia's nuclear arsenal now said to be the greatest on earth, many are sitting up and taking notice. General Albion Knight, former supervisor of United States' nuclear arms program, stated recently that Americans may have only a thousand days of freedom left. When asked in an interview to give the reasons for his conclusion, he replied,

Very simply, from the number of directions steps may be taken by the Soviet Union, or the people associated with them, which could bring us to our knees economically or politically. One of these is the instability of the Middle

East. We came within 12 minutes of losing our economic help in November of 1979 when the Mosque in Mecca was captured by a well-armed, well-trained group of terrorists. They were attempting to capture the King of Saudi Arabia at prayer. They came within 12 minutes of doing it. One of the conditions we know of concerning his release would have been the turning off of all oil shipments from Saudi Arabia to the United States. We would have faced economic disaster within 3 weeks (*Perhaps Today* magazine, Jan.-Feb., 1982, p. 13).

The rise of Russia as a strong military power with designs on the Middle East is no surprise to those acquainted with Bible prophecy. The Prophet Ezekiel wrote about the warlike nature of Russia in the last days and of her invasion of Israel sometime after the establishment of that nation by Jews returning to their ancient homeland.

While Ezekiel used names in his prophecy unfamiliar to many today—Gog, Magog, Meshech, and Tubal—scholars have long identified these as Russia, the aggressor mentioned by Ezekiel. The prophet said,

And the Word of the Lord came unto me, saying, Son of man, set thy face against Gog, the land of Magog, the chief prince of Meshech and Tubal, and prophesy against him, and say, Thus saith the Lord God: Behold, I am against thee, O Gog, the chief prince of Meshech and Tubal: And I will bring thee forth, and all thine army, horses and horsemen, all of them clothed with all sorts of armor, even a great company with bucklers and shields, all of them handling swords: Persia, Ethiopia, Gomer, and all his bands; and many people with thee . . . . After many days thou shalt be visited: in the latter years thou shalt come into the land that is brought back from the sword, and is gathered out of many people, against the mountains of Israel, which have been always waste: but it is brought forth out of many nations, and they shall dwell safely all of them (Ezek. 38:1-6, 8).

While speaking in a series of meetings at a church in Illinois, I announced that my topic for the last service would be "The Coming War with Russia according to the Scriptures." A few days later a member of the church gave me a mimeographed sermon by a former pastor on a similar subject. Thanking my visitor for his thoughtfulness, I went upstairs to the room in the parsonage where I was staying during the meetings. The desk in my room faced a window that overlooked the church cemetery. As I glanced out the window, I was startled to see a large gravestone engraved with the name of the man whose sermon I was about to read. The second shock came when I noticed the date on the first page: the Sunday before Pearl Harbor Day, 1941.

As I read the work of this man of God, I was thrilled with the accuracy of his interpretation and his grasp of then-future events. He had not allowed the news of Hitler's war machine rolling across Europe or the threatening war clouds that would soon engulf the world to drive him to careless predictions. Basing his remarks on Ezekiel 38—39, he explained that Russia would become the major world threat after the war and that finally Israel—not even a nation at that time—would be invaded by the Soviet Union and other nations named in the text.

The preacher was right on target, and his conclusions were shared by others of his time. Dr. H. A. Ironside wrote in *Lectures on Ezekiel*: "In the last days, the final head of the Russian people will look with covetous eyes upon the great developments in the land of Palestine ... and will determine that Russia must have her part in the wealth there produced. Consequently, we have the picture of a vast army, augmented by warriors from Persia, Cush, Phut, marching down toward Palestine" (Loizeaux Bros., p. 267).

But 20th-century students of prophecy were not the first to settle on this now widely accepted interpretation. Two hundred years earlier, Bishop Robert Lowth of London had identified Russia as the end-time aggressor against Israel named by Ezekiel.

What does all this have to do with people's anxiety today? Why do these facts give us the feeling that we are living on the brink of disaster?

People who reject or know nothing about the biblical revelation of Russia's invasion of Israel are likely to be concerned about the future of the world because of the massive military buildup by Russia during the past decade and current reaction to that threat. They fear a nuclear confrontation between the Soviet Union and the United States would destroy both nations. People who do understand and believe Ezekiel's prophecy, however, often suspect that an invasion of the Middle East by Russia would bring about a nuclear war between Russia and the United States because of our ties with Israel and our interests in that part of the world. Neither view is comforting.

Hal Lindsey speculates on this matter in his book *The Late Great Planet Earth.*

It is quite possible that Ezekiel was referring to the U.S. in part when he said: "I will send fire ... on those who dwell securely in the coastlands" (Ezek. 39:6, RSV).

The word translated "coastlands" or "isle" in the Hebrew is *ai*. It was used by the ancients in the sense of "continents" today. It designated the great Gentile civilizations across the seas which were usually settled most densely along the coastlands. The idea here is that the Gentile nations on distant continents would all experience the impact of sudden torrents of fire raining down upon them. This can include prophetically the populated continents and islands of the Western hemisphere as well as the Far East. It pictures cataclysmic events which affect the whole inhabited earth (Zondervan, pp. 161-162).

Lindsey's comments are speculative, of course. The Bible does not reveal America's role in the war between Russia and Israel. Nevertheless, uncertainty in such an explosive climate is enough to cause alarm.

Other Threats

Nuclear war is not the only threat of our time. Crumbling moral foundations and the rise of crime rob many of personal peace. According to the Apostle Paul, greed, violence, and immorality will characterize the last days. He said in his second letter to Timothy:

This know also, that in the last days perilous times shall come, for men shall be lovers of their own selves, covetous, boasters, proud, blasphemers, disobedient to parents, unthankful, unholy, without natural affection, truce breakers, false accusers, incontinent, fierce, despisers of those that are good, traitors, heady, high-minded, lovers of pleasures more than lovers of God; having a form of godliness, but denying the power thereof. From such turn away (3:1-5).

Jesus compared the end time to the days of Noah and to the time of the destruction of Sodom:

And as it was in the days of Noah, so shall it be also in the days of the Son of man. They did eat, they drank, they married wives, they were given in marriage, until the flood came and destroyed them all. Likewise also as it was in the days of Lot. They did eat, they drank, they bought, they sold, they planted, they builded. But the same day that Lot went out of Sodom it rained fire and brimstone and destroyed them all. Even thus shall it be in the day when the Son of man is revealed (Luke 17:26-30).

Statistics on crime and immorality are so well-reported it is unnecessary to repeat them here. But they are staggering. Commenting on crime, former ambassador and congresswoman Clare Boothe Luce said, "Assuming that the present growth rate of crime, alcoholism, drug taking, and commercialized sex persists into 1996, America by then will be the most drunken, drug-soaked, sex-ridden, and criminal society on earth" ("If Present Trends Continue Democracy Is Bound to Collapse," *U.S. News and World Report*, July 5, 1976, pp. 65-66).

To millions, however, living on the brink means a life of economic uncertainty. The huge flow of money to the energy-producing nations has adversely affected the economies of most major nations of the world. As a result, some people expect the most serious economic depression in history to occur in the near future. They fear losing their jobs, their businesses, or their homes.

On the Brink

How is it that the most technically advanced generation of all time stands on the threshold of doom? Where is the utopia that was supposed to follow progressive education and scientific advance? Bible scholar, Carl F. H. Henry has observed,

We applaud modern man's capability but forget that nations are threatening each other with atomic destruction; that gun smoke darkens our inner cities, and that our near neighbors walk in terror by day and sleep in fear by night. We sit glued to television sets, unmindful that ancient pagan rulers staged colosseum circuses to switch the minds of the restless ones from the realities of a spiritually vagrant empire to the illusion that all was well. Today, some are still glued. Others are coming unglued.

We are perched collectively on a precipice and becoming more aware of our precarious position each day. A quiet panic is spreading across the land. Technology has failed to provide us with security. After taking a giant step for mankind, we seem to be limping fearfully toward destruction.

What is the answer for this generation?

Is there a refuge from the storms that are sweeping in on us?

Is there a place to hide?

2 FORTRESS OVER THE HILLTOP

Thousands of Americans are getting ready to head for the hills. These concerned people, calling themselves "survivalists," believe they can outlast the coming disaster and social collapse by hiding away till the worst is over. In his article "Apocalypse Now?" Ernest Volkman said of the survivalists:

To them the future is a nightmare vision. Society, which they already feel is far past redemption, will one day totally collapse, either because general nuclear war will have broken out or because the stresses and strains now tearing at the American fabric will finally rip it apart. They believe that when that day comes, millions of crazed, starving (or perhaps radiation-burned) people, mostly from the cities, will wander America, desperately scouring for food, water, and shelter—and possibly killing anyone who stands in their way. And when that inevitable day comes, the only survivors will be those who prepared—starting now. (*Family Weekly*, Nov. 8, 1981, p. 8).

One's first impression of the survivalists may be that they are typical extremists or social dropouts. Some are. But the majority of survivalists are middle-class Americans running scared.

Survivalists can be found among businessmen, manufacturers, professional people, farmers—a general cross section of the population. Special Correspondent Peter Arnett of the Associated Press wrote,

Small but growing bands of Americans are arming themselves and learning how to kill because they are convinced the social order is crumbling and they will have to fend for themselves to survive.

They are attached neither to hate groups nor to political groups. They include middle Americans who are remortgaging their homes to pay for guns and shooting lessons for their families, and professional men accumulating arsenals in their homes and strongholds scattered through southeastern woodlands, midwestern suburbs, remote western ranches, and mountainside cabins in the Pacific Northwest ("Survivalists Armed, Ready for the Worst," *Detroit Free Press*, Mar. 2, 1981).

Many survivalists are devoutly religious; some are professing Christians. The word "Christian" appears in the names of some of the survivalist groups—one group requires that its members be male, Christian, and property owners.

No one knows how large the survivalist movement is, but a clue to its size can be found by examining the lucrative survival supplies business.

One California-based distributor has built a million dollar business selling freeze-dried coffee and other food items. More exotic wares, such as radiation suits and night vision glasses costing thousands of dollars, are also offered to survivalists. A number of new magazines cater to this growing segment of the population, and manuals and books on the subject are selling by the thousands.

Everyone Is a Survivalist

To some degree we are all survivalists. We work to provide food, clothing, and shelter for ourselves and our families. The medical profession is dedicated to the survival of human beings. Farmers produce food to make it possible for everyone else to survive. Even the Bible writers commanded us to labor diligently in order to survive in difficult times. Laziness because of lack of interest in preparing for the future is condemned:

Go to the ant, thou sluggard; consider her ways, and be wise: which having no guide, overseer, or ruler, provideth her meat in the summer, and gathereth her food in the harvest. How long wilt thou sleep, O sluggard? When wilt thou arise out of they sleep? Yet a little sleep, a little slumber, a little folding of the hands to sleep: so shall thy poverty come as one that travelleth, and thy want as an armed man (Prov. 6:6-11).

Paul uses strong language to correct the idea that Christians can neglect the material needs of their families and still be in the will of God. He said of these deceived people: "But if any provide not for his own, and specially for those of his own house, he hath denied the faith, and is worse than an infidel" (1 Tim. 5:8). He prescribes the following for lazy ones in the fellowship at Thessalonica: "If any would not work, neither should he eat" (2 Thes. 3:10).

Survivalism and Violence

Christian leaders are generally reacting negatively to the survivalist movement for a number of reasons.

The greatest concern expressed by those who have researched survivalism is its preoccupation with paramilitarism. Many survivalists are armed to the teeth and are continually working on their marksmanship, fully expecting to someday use their weapons on other people. One company is doing very well selling small submachine guns to survivalists.

The spread of survivalism is creating a potentially volatile situation, with scores of armed camps willing to fight for what each thinks is vital to survival. If survivalism is the great growth movement of the '80s, as some predict, we could be on the doorstep of guerrilla warfare. The movement intended to save us may, in fact, destroy us without any aid from foreign enemies.

Many survivalists are serious about destroying anyone who might want some of their cache of food and supplies.

This raises the question: What is the Christian's responsibility when he has food and others are starving? The answer is clear. The writer of Proverbs said, "Say not unto thy neighbor, 'Go, and come again, and tomorrow I will give; when thou hast it by thee' " (Prov. 3:27). "He that withholdeth corn, the people shall curse him: but blessing shall be upon the head of him that selleth it" (Prov. 11:26). And Jesus said, "Thou shalt love thy neighbor as thyself" (Matt. 19:19).

Even when the needy are enemies, Christians are to respond with generosity: "Therefore if thine enemy hunger, feed him, if he thirst, give him drink" (Rom. 12:20).

These may be difficult teachings to follow in extreme circumstances, but they are in the Bible and hard survivalists who profess to be Christians ought to face up to them. (Hard survivalists are the gun-toting kind. Soft survivalists simply store up food and supplies in the event of a catastrophe of some kind.)

Survivalism and Stewardship
We are stewards of cents and seconds, and someday we must face our record. The Apostle Paul wrote, "So then every one of us shall give an account of himself to God"

(Rom. 14:12). "For we must all appear before the Judgment Seat of Christ, that every one may receive the things done in his body, according to that he hath done, whether it be good or bad" (2 Cor. 5:10).

Many people in the survivalist movement spend as much money, time, and effort on their fortress or bunker retreats as on their homes. But can one justify thousands of dollars of investment in a wilderness hideaway when people are starving for food and for the Gospel? Can one feel right about spending uncounted hours in training camps and weapons proficiency while neglecting his responsibility in the body of Christ?

But, you say, this is a matter of life and death ... of survival.

Perhaps.

We are not sure that the dire predictions of the panic peddlers will come true. And if they do, it is unlikely that survival will be possible in a nuclear holocaust—even in a fortress hideaway.

Survivalism and the Purposes of God

There is another dimension to this dilemma: How does the survivalist approach to life square with the purposes of God for His people? An Old Testament text (1 Kings 19) may provide an answer to this important question.

The chapter opens with the news that Elijah the prophet has just received word that Queen Jezebel has vowed she will have him executed. Elijah's first thought is survival. He runs for his life. Forty-one days later, Elijah is still alive and hiding in a cave. The whole ordeal has been a soul-wrenching experience for the prophet. He has never lacked courage, but now he has allowed survival to become more important than service. He is a defeated man, cowering in a cave, expecting to die.

While in his survival hideaway, Elijah heard God ask, "What doest thou here, Elijah?" (19:9) The prophet stated his case: "I have been very jealous for the Lord God of hosts, for the Children of Israel have forsaken Thy covenant, thrown down Thine altars, and slain Thy prophets with the sword; and I, even I only, am left; and they seek my life, to take it away" (19:10). Then everything broke loose. A great wind broke rocks in pieces. On the tail of the wind was an earthquake. Scarcely had the earth stopped trembling beneath the prophet's feet when a fire flared up before his eyes. After the fire, Elijah heard a still small voice asking the same question he had heard before: "What doest thou here, Elijah?" (19:13)

Elijah was hiding in a cave, trying to survive, and fearing death, yet he was to be one of only two men who would not die. Like Enoch, Elijah would be taken to heaven without experiencing physical death. His fears of death were never realized; his future was brighter than he could have imagined.

The prophet finally left his survival hideaway and began to serve his Lord again. There was much to do: he was commissioned to anoint a king and to choose a replacement for himself. Elijah once again became a man on the move in the work of God. In the one weak period of his life, Elijah learned that the safest place to be and the surest place to survive is in the center of the heavenly Father's will. His feelings of fear and defeat had been needless.

Christians are people with a mission. We have important work to do: divine service. If we spend our time, energy, and money preparing for disasters that may not even occur, we will not be effective in our God-given tasks. Fear will limit our usefulness and rob us of blessings and rewards we could have possessed if we had kept our priorities right.

Survivalism and Fear

Survivalists take great care in locating their fortress hideaways in "safe" locations, calculated by studying the proximity of nuclear targets such as military bases, missile silos, and large cities, the frequency of tornadoes and earthquakes, and climate.

Most survivalists prefer the mountainous regions of the West. Others like the Southeast. One group has even proposed a "golden triangle of safety" in the Midwest to which all Americans who want to survive should go when it becomes necessary.

All of these proposals call for living on the perimeter of panic. One survivalist in Oregon refuses to drive more than a gas tank's distance from his rural home lest an emergency cut him off from his arsenal. Such an attitude not only restricts activity and limits influence and outreach but is foreign to every principle of the Christian message.

The just are to live by faith (Rom. 1:17), and fear is the opposite of faith. As faith increases, fear decreases. We are not corralled by fear if we live in the circle of God's love. To understand this is to be free. The Apostle John said, "There is no fear in love; but perfect love casteth out fear: because fear hath torment. He that feareth is not made perfect in love" (1 John 4:18).

It is especially sad when people ruled by fears are limited by anxieties over events that never materialize. Yet many fears fall into that category. How many times have you fretted over something that never happened? C. H. Spurgeon wrote, "Fear hath many eyes, and yet trembles at what it does not see. We look through the telescope of apprehension, breathe on the glass, and think we see clouds, when indeed it is only our anxious breath."

No one can be sure that the doomsday predictions driving

people to the hills and hideaways of rural America will happen in our lifetime. It is tragic, then, when time and substance are invested in elaborate plans for survival instead of being used to carry the message of Christ and His love to lost people in our country and around the world. Eternal preparations deserve priority.

Shared Views

Christians do hold some views in common with survivalists. We agree that these are perilous times. We acknowledge the awful possibility of nuclear war. We are aware of the militaristic stance of Russia. We know that natural disasters are likely to increase.

The difference between Christians and survivalists should be in their reactions to these realities. Survivalists retreat. Christians are to be advancing with the Gospel. Survivalists narrow their circumference of activity. Christians are always to be enlarging their outreach. Survivalists are building strongholds. Christians are to be attacking the strongholds of sin.

Survivalists are improving their expertise with weapons that destroy, expecting to even fight off their neighbors in a coming disaster. Christians are to be constantly improving their effectiveness with the spiritual weapons of faith and prayer to overcome evil and to benefit their communities. Paul wrote, "For the weapons of our warfare are not carnal, but mighty through God to the pulling down of strongholds, casting down imaginations, and every high thing that exalteth itself against the knowledge of God, and bringing into captivity every thought to the obedience of Christ" (2 Cor. 10:4-5).

Survivalists recognize man's violent nature. Christians also recognize the sinful and violent nature of man, but are to share the message that imparts a new nature: "Therefore if any man be in Christ, he is a new creature; old things are passed away; behold all things are become new. And all things are of God, who hath reconciled us to Himself by Jesus Christ, and hath given to us the ministry of reconciliation" (2 Cor. 5:17-18).

Survivalists are digging in. Christians are to be looking up: "And when these things begin to come to pass, then look up, and lift up your heads; for your redemption draweth nigh" (Luke 21:28).

Survivalists are troubled people, always glancing to the hills where they can retreat and feel safe when trouble comes. Christians have been instructed to put trouble out of their hearts. They know there is no place on earth as safe as the center of their Father's will. In the final analysis, their survival rests with Him.

3 SWISS BANKS AND BURIED TREASURE

There are two concepts of survival. One is coming through alive; the other, coming through rich. Thousands of Americans have decided to become rich and are investing in and storing precious metals in what they hope are safe places. Many of these investors believe they will emerge from a future disaster financially secure because of their foresight. The Bible reveals that these financial precautions will be in vain. James said, "Go to now, ye rich men, weep and howl for your miseries shall come upon you. Your riches are corrupted, and your garments are moth-eaten. Your gold and silver is cankered: and the rust of them shall be a witness against you, and shall eat your flesh as it were fire. Ye have heaped treasure together for the last days" (James 5:1-3).

In unknowing fulfillment of this prophecy, people are converting their treasures into many forms and stashing them in unusual places. Some are hiding their savings in jars buried or hidden on their property while others are constructing concrete safes or opening bank accounts in Switzerland.

Why all these precautions? The most likely reason seems to be the fear of a coming economic crash that will make dollars worthless and banks unable to cover the deposits of their customers. This kind of thinking commonly floats around in times of economic uncertainty, but is now being encouraged by a number of writers who specialize in forecasting economic gloom.

The Doomsayers

In *How to Prosper during the Coming Bad Years*, author Howard J. Ruff says:

> The purpose of this book is to persuade you that the United States is about to enter its greatest test period since the Civil War—an inflationary spiral leading to a depression that will be remembered with a shudder for generations.

> No one knows exactly where the breaking point is, but it's coming, and soon. As this book is published, America is truly on the brink, and so is the rest of the world, because when we sneeze, the rest of the world gets pneumonia (Times Books, p. 12).

Ruff predicts exploding inflation, price controls, erosion of savings, and an international monetary crisis that will destroy all paper currency.

Is there any possibility of avoiding such a crash? Not according to Ruff. He writes, "The juggernaut is heading for the precipice, and it doesn't matter whether we go soaring over the cliff with our foot on the accelerator (inflation), or skidding with our foot on the brake (deflation)" (p. 12).

Doug Clark, author of *How to Survive the Money Crash*, not only expects a deep depression, but thinks it has been planned by a group of conspirators. He explains: "The depression is planned. It is going to be coordinated and orchestrated to a superlative degree with other conspiratorial plans, all leading to the deterioration of the will of the people of the United States and the death of the sovereignty of the United States, for all intents and purposes" (Harvest House, p. 112).

Clark, believing there will be a rash of bank failures, lists 10 developments to signal his readers to rush to their banks and withdraw their money.

Geoffery F. Abert, author of *After the Crash*, expects some catastrophic event will be the straw that breaks the economy's back. He thinks this final straw may be the bankruptcy of several large banks, the default of two or three cities on bond obligations, a nationwide paralysis of transportation and communication, a series of natural disasters, or nuclear blackmail by some minor power (Signet Books, p. 75).

And Doug Casey warns in his bestselling book *Crisis Investing*, "The financial waters, both here and abroad, are troubled now. I am convinced that gale-force winds will soon hit us followed by tidal waves of panic and collapse" (Pocket Books, p. 7). Casey foresees an economic crunch that will result in riots, protests, and crime in the streets as people try to find someone to blame for the problems besetting them.

Silver and Gold

Convinced of the certainty of a future great depression that will make currency worthless and banks treasure traps, most prophets of economic doom recommend alternative survival methods such as putting savings in Swiss banks and investing in silver and gold. Doug Clark even advises selling one's home in order to invest the money in these precious metals (Clark, *How to Survive*, p. 141).

But where does one keep large quantities of gold or silver? Clark tells his readers that the best place for these metals is a home-safe cemented into the floor; second best is a spot in a wall or floor known only to the investor. Both should be wired with an alarm system hooked up to the local police station.

All this gives cause to pause and think. Is there really a safe safe? Or a safe substance?

It is not surprising that people today think gold is enduring. This coveted metal has historically held its value while currency has fluctuated with political and economic fortunes. Man's interest in gold goes back to ancient times—gold as a precious metal is mentioned in Genesis 2:11-12. The search for gold has continued through the centuries. Many have risked life and limb to obtain it. But valuable as gold is, it will someday betray its holders: "Your gold and silver is cankered; and the rust of them shall be a witness against you, and shall eat your flesh as it were fire. Ye have heaped treasure together for the last days" (James 5:3).

What would cause gold to lose its value? We do not know. Perhaps a devaluation will be the result of a worldwide acceptance of a yet unknown currency. It is a fact that strong currencies cause the value of gold to decline and weak currencies make gold valuable. A currency that seems absolutely stable may therefore rob gold of its value in the future.

Another factor in the end time depreciation of gold may be conditions that make people face up to real values. Since precious metals do not have life-sustaining qualities, they lose their value quickly when life is threatened. Tons of gold are worthless to a starving man during a severe food shortage. In a survival situation, wealth measured under normal circumstances is of little value.

There are other reasons for the devaluation of precious metals.

Students of prophecy as well as some economists expect a cashless society. The technology to make such a move possible is already with us. In this system, earnings and assets are transferred to a central computer bank from which withdrawals are made at checkout counters in stores and other places of business. Proponents of a moneyless economy point out such a system would eliminate theft and lower personal injuries often associated with crime. Biblical reasons for anticipating such a development are based on the prophesied "mark of the beast" that will be required for all business transactions during the reign of the Antichrist: "And he causeth all, both small and great, rich and poor, free and bond, to receive a mark in their right hand, or in their foreheads; and that no man might buy or sell, save he that had the mark, or the name of the beast, or the number of his name" (Rev. 13:16-17).

With the establishment of a cashless society, a powerful government could call in all precious metals at a value determined by those in control. Under such conditions, the hoarding of gold or silver would probably become a crime.

Another view is that uncontrolled inflation coupled with price ceilings on gold and silver may quickly erode the wealth of those who invested in these metals.

Inflation and deflation are thieves that cannot be locked out of concrete vaults or avoided by the use of foreign bank accounts.

Other Uncertainties
We cannot be sure a great depression will occur—none is prophesied in the Bible. The stockpiling of commodities and cash may all be unnecessary. Nor do we know when Christ will return, but the proximity of that event does not mean the economies of the world will fall apart.

On the contrary, biblical prophecies seem to indicate the last days will be days of economic boom. Jesus revealed that the countdown years would be like those preceding the Flood. They were anything but depression years. Instead, the fast-living and affluent antediluvians were too busy eating and drinking to be bothered by Noah's message before the Flood came and destroyed them all.

The conditions in Sodom just before its destruction are also said to have been similar to those that will exist in the last days. Note our Lord's description of that time: "Likewise also as it was in the days of Lot; they did eat, they drank, they bought, they sold, they planted, they builded. But the same day that Lot went out of Sodom it rained fire from heaven and destroyed them all. Even thus shall it be in the day when the Son of man is revealed" (Luke 17:28-30).

So it appears that those who store gold and silver in favorite hiding places while awaiting catastrophe will be doubly disappointed. Their margin of safety will collapse while the general world economy will roar along in unexpected health, turning people's minds increasingly to materialism.

But a word of caution is needed. Economists differ. Fortunes still may be made or lost through wise or unwise investments, even in precious metals. Time is the all-important factor. Where are we in time? How near is the return of the Lord? When will end time hoarders lose it all? When will the gold and silver crash come? No one knows for certain.

Certainties

While there is no safe hiding place for our earthly treasures, we can use them to make eternal investments that will never depreciate and cannot be touched by thieves. Jesus said, "Lay not up for yourselves treasures upon earth, where moth and rust doth corrupt, and where thieves break through and steal, but lay up for yourselves treasures in heaven, where neither moth nor rust doth corrupt, and where thieves do not break through nor steal" (Matt. 6:19-20).

Heavenly investments also deepen our spiritual lives: "For where your treasure is, there will your heart be also" (6:21). One dimension to heavenly investments is their availability to all believers, regardless of their financial reserves. Most earthly investments require considerable capital. Many who read about hiding gold or opening Swiss bank accounts can never do so because they have little of this world's wealth. If their survival depends on holding gold or making foreign investments, they have no hope at all.

Gifts to the Lord's work, one way of investing in heavenly treasure, are not rewarded because of their size but according to the ability of the giver. Jesus said that the poor widow who cast her two mites into the temple treasury had given more than the rich men who had given large gifts: "Of a truth I say unto you, that this poor widow hath cast in more than they all: for all these have of their abundance cast in unto the offerings of God; but she of her penury hath cast in all the living she had" (Luke 21:3-4). George Mueller, the Englishman who trusted God to feed and clothe his orphans, said; "God judges what we give by what we keep" (Walter B. Knight, *Knight's Treasury of Illustrations*, Eerdmans, p. 139). A Christian businessman once told me with evident pride that he was to have lunch with a millionaire who had been converted to Christianity. He said this wealthy convert had bequested large sums of money to Christian causes. I wondered about that.

How much is a heavenly investment worth when it is made with money we do not need while living?

This is not to question the motives of those who live on dividends while planning to put the capital to work for Christ after they have gone to heaven. But can one cling to a fortune here below, living like a king, and still expect a crown for bequeathing his holdings to the Lord's work after he is through with them?

A man once contributed the funds needed to build a church and later lost all of his property.

"If you had the money you put into that church," someone said to him, "you could start again."

The man replied, "That is the only money I have saved. If I had not given it to the Lord it would have gone with the rest. Now it will always be mine" (Walter B. Knight, *Knight's Master Book of New Illustrations*, Eerdmans, p. 251).

Charles Spurgeon advised, "Never try to save out of God's cause; such money will canker the rest. Giving to God is no loss; it is putting your substance in the best bank. Giving is true having, as the old gravestone said of the dead man: 'What I spent I had; what I saved I lost; what I gave I have'" (Knight, *Knight's Master Book*, p. 242). An epitaph on a simple monument in St. Paul's Cathedral in London reads: "Sacred to the memory of Charles George Gordon, who at all times and everywhere gave his strength to the weak, his substance to the poor, his sympathy to the suffering, his heart to God" (Knight, *Knight's Master Book*, p. 239).

So there is an investment that endures. All of earth's hiding places are suspect. Thieves may find and steal your buried treasure. Foreign banks may fail. The price of precious metals may plummet. Your savings may be devoured by inflation or lost in a crash.

But the portion you give to God will be safe.

4 A CHRISTIAN POLITICAL SOLUTION?

Not everyone can head for the hills. The fortress fad is for the financially able. Nor can everyone invest in precious metals or store up large amounts of money in foreign bank accounts. If survival depends on these expensive means, most people will perish.

Is there another way?

Many American Christians are convinced that there are political answers to the problems of the nation and the world. Since righteousness exalts a nation (Prov. 14:34), why not enact laws and elect candidates dedicated to righteous living?

The idea is catching on. Political action is now supported by some churches that once avoided it at all costs. They insisted that preaching the Gospel was their reason for existing and that any church involvement in politics to bring about social change constituted an adoption of the social gospel. These churches have given priority to converting the lost and building up believers in the faith. They have spoken out strongly on moral issues such as abortion, sexual permissiveness, and homosexuality because these practices violate biblical teachings, but have shunned political issues and identification with any candidate or political party.

Times have changed. We have entered an era in which some Christian leaders believe it is their duty to call on churches to exert pressure on the leaders of government in nearly every area of political thought and action.

The speaker at a ministers' conference which I attended urged his listeners to honor acceptable candidates in church services in order to expose these politicians to their congregations. Even the presence of the politician's automobile (with its campaign stickers) in the church parking lot would be intended to have a beneficial impact on passersby.

This about face in the role of churches in political action raises a number of questions: Is this move into the political arena by churches and other religious organizations a new direction in the will of God for His people, or is it an adaptation of the old social gospel? Will closer ties between the church and the government prove beneficial or detrimental to both? Will the election of political candidates endorsed by Christian leaders move us closer to world peace?

These questions may be best answered by raising four more: What has happened in the past when the church has courted favor with the state? What is the mission of the church? What is God's method of change? When will world peace come?

The Church and the State
Our Lord made it clear that there should always be a separation between the church and the state: "Render therefore unto Caesar the things which are Caesar's; and unto God the things that are God's" (Matt. 22:21). Yet Christians are to be obedient to the laws of the state: "Submit yourselves to every ordinance of man for the Lord's sake whether it be

to the king, as supreme, or unto governors, as unto them that are sent by Him for the punishment of evildoers and for the praise of them that do well" (1 Peter 2:13-14). The only exceptions to this rule are situations where the law of the state calls for disobedience to a teaching of the Bible. In these cases the Law of God prevails. Peter reflected this attitude when he said, "We ought to obey God rather than men" (Acts 5:29).

Following this principle, the early Christians overcame seemingly insurmountable obstacles and carried the Gospel to all parts of their world. Bitter opposition from government and religious leaders complicated their task, and the price of progress was often imprisonment and death. Witness the New Testament record of conquests and casualties. Peter and John were imprisoned and beaten shortly after Pentecost (Acts 4:3; 5:40). Stephen was stoned to death for his preaching, and became the first Christian martyr (Acts 7:57-60). James the brother of John was slain by Herod and shortly thereafter Peter was imprisoned again (Acts 12:1-5). All of the apostles, with the exception of John who was banished to the Isle of Patmos, were martyred.

Persecution continued long after the Apostolic Age ended. When nearly half of Rome burned, Emperor Nero blamed the fire on innocent Christians and vented his fury on them. Some were sewed up in the skins of wild animals and then attacked by savage dogs. Others, wrapped in tow and smeared with tar, were fastened to tall poles in the palace garden and set on fire while Nero, attended by his slaves and courtiers, reclined on a balcony and watched his "torches" (John Foxe, *Foxe's Christian Martyrs of the World*, Moody Press, p. 38). The colosseum in Rome became the last earthly stop for many Christians as Roman citizens gathered to see them attacked by wild beasts and criminals.

But persecution did not stop the church. The blood of the

martyrs became its seed. The church was united and purified, spurred on to greater accomplishments.

What persecution could not do, however, was accomplished by the marriage of the church to the Roman government. After 300 years of triumph, the church was tamed through compromise. In A.D. 313 the Emperor Constantine professed to have seen a vision that converted him to Christianity. He ordered his troops to carry the Christian insignia and the persecution of the church ended.

The church, now recognized and welcomed by the government, began to wield power in the affairs of the state and Roman emperors began to influence the affairs of the church.

It seemed to have won a great victory, but its union with the state brought severe defeats.

In his book *The Church in History*, B. K. Kuiper describes that era:

The Christian name now secured many and great material advantages. The Christian name had become a passport to political, military, and social promotion. As a result, thousands upon thousands of heathen joined the church.

Unfortunately many of these were Christians in name only. The Christianity of Emperor Constantine himself was, if not doubtful, at least not of a very high character. What the church gained in quantity it lost in quality. Constantine's edict of 313 opened the floodgates through which a mighty stream of corruption poured into the church (Eerdmans, p. 27).

The union formed by Constantine continued to plague both the church and the state through the centuries, bringing spiritual dearth and political oppression. When Christians began to use carnal means to advance the cause of Christ, the real mission of the church was stifled.

Kuiper further explains that "during the first three centuries the church was extended by peaceful means. The victory over heathenism was won not by fighting but by enduring suffering. After 313, Christians at times employed the methods of war to advance their cause. The emblem of the Roman armies had been the eagle. The eagle was now replaced by the cross" (Kuiper, *The Church*, p. 27).

In yielding to the temptation to exert political power, the church lost its spiritual power. Dreams of transforming the Roman Empire into a model Christian political entity were never realized. Instead of the government being purified by the church, the church was corrupted by the government. There is no reason to believe that the unequal yoke of political and religious power will be less harmful to the cause of Christ today.

The Mission of the Church

The basic mission of the church is capsuled in what we know as the Great Commission: "And Jesus came and spake unto them, saying, 'All power is given unto Me in heaven and in earth. Go ye therefore, and teach all nations, baptizing them in the name of the Father, and the Son, and of the Holy Ghost, teaching them to observe all things whatsoever I have commanded you. And lo, I am with you alway, even unto the end of the world' " (Matt. 28:18-20).

From the earliest days of the church these marching orders have sent Christians forth with one message: Christ died, was buried and rose again, according to the Scriptures (1 Cor. 15:1-4). This is the Gospel; it is the unchanging message that changes the lives of those who respond to it in faith.

Local churches are intended to be more than corporate groups that meet to hold services, take offerings, pay bills, and put together programs to combat social and political evils. They are to be worship and training centers for maturing believers who then go forth to do the work of the ministry (Eph. 4:11-16). Each Christian should be so enriched by his church that he is able to take the Gospel to others in love and spiritually reproduce himself in them.

Does this mean that churches should be silent about wrongs in their membership and evil in the world? Certainly not. Our Lord called His followers to be the salt of the earth and the light of the world (Matt. 5:13-14). The Holy Spirit uses the church as a force against evil: "For the mystery of iniquity doth already work: only he who now letteth [hindereth] will let [hinder], until he be taken out of the way" (2 Thes. 2:7).

The church must stand against evil. But can this be best accomplished by adding a political dimension to the mission given to the church? Not if history is any guide. The church has been most effective when sticking tenaciously to its biblical message.

It has been said that the secret of John Wesley's power was his kingly neglect of trifles as he mastered the important thing—the preaching of the Gospel.

All power in heaven and on earth is provided for proclaiming the Gospel. This is not true of any other message. Political ideas and convictions come and go. Sometimes they even float from one political party to another so that after a time one group has almost switched positions with the other.

The Gospel remains the same.

When a church neglects the Gospel or relegates it to second place in favor of a political message, it has departed from a lasting message and embraced a passing one. The emphasis of that church has moved from the eternal to the temporal, a change of direction that will ultimately bring decline.

There are other dangers. Politicians are notoriously unwilling or unable to keep many of the promises they make to win votes. In the heat of a political campaign, rhetoric sometimes outdistances reason or honesty. When a candidate is elected because his political positions please church leaders who publicly support him, the credibility of these leaders and their church is on the line right along with that of the politician.

The eyes of the nation watch those elected through Christians' efforts and if the politicians renege on their promises and responsibilities, churches stand to lose points for lack of discernment. For example, economic setbacks may be blamed on churches that have given their support to a candidate even though economic policies may not have been the reason churches supported the candidate.

If church-supported candidates lose an election, the community may question the influence and power of the church. Sometimes these candidates are the object of much prayer by the church and victory is expected through divine intervention. A loss then may not only demoralize the church but cast doubt on the power of prayer.

A minister who had given enthusiastic support to a politician who lost the election groaned, "What am I going to do now?"

"I guess you'll just have to go back to preaching the Gospel," one of his board members replied.

Political victory is perhaps more dangerous to churches than is loss. The taste of winning and the thrill of gaining power can plunge a church even deeper into political action and cause it to neglect its God-given mission.

Of all the periods of history, ours may cry the loudest for the church to return to its task. It is time to get back to the basics.

God's Method of Change
God changes society one person at a time. Mass evangelism and the use of modern media may turn millions to Christ,

but they all come to the Lord individually. On the Day of Pentecost, 3,000 individuals came to faith in Christ. The city of Nineveh was moved to repentance citizen by citizen, including the king. "So the people of Nineveh believed God, and proclaimed a fast, and put on sackcloth from the greatest of them to the least of them. For the word came unto the King of Nineveh, and he arose from his throne, and he laid his robe from him, and covered him with sackcloth, and sat in ashes" (Jonah 3:5-6). Jesus said, "For God so loved the world, that He gave His only begotten Son, that whosoever believeth in Him should not perish, but have everlasting life" (John 3:16).

Though the mission of the church is to proclaim the Gospel, it does not prohibit individual Christians from seeking political office and promoting righteousness on all levels of the government. Good government springs from good living, but lasting change comes from changed hearts.

William Jennings Bryan, former Secretary of State and Christian statesman, said he had concluded that "Christ's Gospel is the sure cure for all social and political evils" (Walter B. Knight, *Three Thousand Illustrations for Christian Service*, Eerdmans, p. 319). He believed the best method of promoting temperance, social morality, and good citizenship was to bring men to Christ.

Mr. Bryan's up-to-date and biblically sound observation is still good advice for churches that want to change their communities, the nation, and the world.

World Peace

In his last speech before Parliament as Prime Minister, Sir Winston Churchill gloomily said: "Which way can we turn to save our lives and the future of the world? It does not matter so much to old people. They are going soon anyway. But I find it poignant to look at youth in all its activity and ardor, and most of all, to watch little children playing their many games, and wonder what would lie before them if God wearied of mankind" (Walter B. Knight, *Knight's Up-to-the-Minute Illustrations*, Moody Press, p. 178).

There will be no Christian political solution to the problem of peace for the nation and the world till Christ returns to establish His kingdom. This does not mean that Christians should sit idly by while their communities and country need their wisdom and abilities. It does not mean that believers should fold their hands and let the world fall apart when they can do something to help solve problems.

God will not lay aside His eternal plan that ultimately includes world peace. But today He invites people to receive eternal life through faith in His Son. He is changing people who in turn can have a positive impact on their communities. Believers who are wise will give priority to this most important effort while time remains.

5 OF MISSILES AND MEN

Nuclear war is unthinkable, yet many are thinking about it. After a period of relative calm known as detente, the nuclear war issue has exploded again. Articles and books describing the nightmare of nuclear attack appear with increasing regularity.

In their new book, *Energy, Vulnerability, and War*, Wilson Clark and Jake Page focus on Baytown, Texas to dramatize the possibility of nuclear attacks on the energy centers of America. Their hair-raising description is based on a scenario prepared by the Congressional Office of Technology. They write:

In Baytown, there was an explosive blast, driving air away from the site of the explosion—producing what is called static overpressure (a sudden change in air pressure that can crush objects) and high winds, called dynamic pressure, that can move objects suddenly or knock them down. Most of the large buildings in Baytown collapsed because of the static overpressure; it was dynamic pressure that killed most of the people in the vicinity by blowing them into other objects. Walls of two-story houses four miles from the blast were pushed over by pressures of about 180 tons; people were blown away by winds of 160 miles per hour. All of this in seconds.

Again, within seconds of the blast, Baytown was a raging inferno of fire, caused by the blast's heat and the chain-letter effect of petroleum installations collapsing and catching on fire with incendiary power. The sky over Baytown was red; the vast acres of refineries, pipes, and tanks were destroyed—leaking oil into nearby waterways that were themselves burned, incinerating barges and tankers, and leaking poisons from the devastated petrochemical plants into the water and into the surrounding hell that had been Baytown (Norton, p. 31).

Envisioning the Results

In his article "On the Eve of Destruction," Michael Betzold envisions the results of a one-megaton nuclear explosion 6,500 feet above Detroit. Though a one-megaton bomb (equivalent to 1 million tons of TNT) is small by today's standards, it is 80 times more powerful than the bomb dropped on Hiroshima in 1945. Betzold says it is optimistic to speak of a single one-megaton bomb being used because the Soviets have hundreds of much larger nuclear weapons aimed at every major city in the United States.

Betzold further states that even this mini-bomb would create a fireball over Detroit that would burn at 100 million degrees centigrade, 15 times the temperature of the surface of the sun. He speaks of melting glass, evaporating steel, exploding concrete, and crumbling buildings. Betzold summarizes, "One day after being hit by a single, relatively tiny nuclear bomb, the city of Detroit is an unbroken expanse of rubble and skeletons. There are 300,000 dead" (*Detroit Magazine*, Detroit Free Press, Jan. 3, 1982, p. 8).

Is Nuclear War Prophesied?

Ezekiel's description of a storm of fire—this one halting Russian invasion of Israel in the last days—has prompted some commentators to conclude that the prophet referred to a coming nuclear war when he wrote, "And I will plead against him with pestilence and with blood; and I will rain upon him, and upon his bands, and upon the many people that are with him, an overflowing rain, and great hailstones, fire, and brimstone" (Ezek. 38:22).

Some of the judgments prophesied in the Book of Revelation also sound strangely like descriptions of nuclear destruction. Here is an example: "The first angel sounded, and there followed hail and fire mingled with blood, and they were cast upon the earth, and the third part of trees was burnt up, and all green grass was burnt up" (Rev. 8:7).

Has technology given man the ability to produce his own apocalypse?

Epidemic of Fear

Endtime destruction does not, of course, rule out God's role in the plagues and judgments of the coming Tribulation period. But our current capacity for the Apocalypse helps us understand some of the reasons for the prophesied epidemic of fear in the last days: "And there shall be signs in the sun, and in the moon, and in the stars; and upon the earth distress of nations, with perplexity; the sea and the waves roaring, men's hearts failing them for fear, and for looking after those things which are coming on the earth: for the powers of heaven shall be shaken" (Luke 21:25-26).

Fear in America is fanned by the Soviet Union's enormous nuclear buildup during the past decade. Russia seems to hold the edge in apocalyptic power, leaving the United States in an uncomfortable position.

What can be done?

To many the answer is simple: We must outgun our adversary. Hundreds of billions of dollars must be poured into the development and manufacture of even more powerful nuclear weapons. Researchers must push on to a breakthrough that will produce the ultimate killer. The size and efficiency of our armed forces must be increased and vastly improved. The nation must be mobilized for war. No cost is too high and no sacrifice too great if the survival of the nation is at stake.

Some object to the armed-to-the-teeth approach. They cite the overkill capacity of both sides—the six nuclear nations together possess the equivalent of five tons of TNT for every person on earth. They see little value in increasing this ratio, pointing out that the United States has more than 1,000 Intercontinental Ballistic Missiles, a sizeable bombing force, and 41 Poseidon submarines, any one of which is capable of destroying every major city in the Soviet Union. Why then keep building more and more nuclear weapons?

Who is correct in this life or death issue? National defense is certainly necessary and even biblical. Israel often overcame her foes by force because God enabled her to do so. The psalmist insisted that God had taught his hands to war (Ps. 18:34).

While we are to love our enemies (Matt. 5:44) and feed them when they are hungry (Rom. 12:20), there is no hint in Scripture that God expects us to give our families over to hostile forces. If neglecting to provide food and clothing for our loved ones is contrary to God's will, how much more the surrender of these family members to a brutal enemy.

Where does national or personal defense end and nuclear lunacy begin? Stockpiling nuclear weapons, even in the name of national defense, carries the risk of war breaking out by accident. Twice in 1980 the United States came close to launching its missiles because of computer error.

This draws attention to another terrifying development: As nuclear weapons become more sophisticated, major nuclear powers depend more on machines for decision-making. While safeguards are built into this system, no computer-controlled response can be flawless. The fate of millions rests on computer accuracy in the event of a real or perceived attack by either side.

We seem to be caught between a rock and a hard place. We are reminded that if we do not have enough nuclear weapons, we may invite war through weakness. On the other hand, we are advised that escalating the arms race may provoke a like response by the other side, increasing the possibility of nuclear confrontation or an accidental war.

Is There a Christian Alternative?

At the close of World War II, General Douglas MacArthur proposed a different dimension to the question of survival in the nuclear age.

We have had our last chance. If we will not devise some great and more equitable system, Armageddon will be at our door. The problem basically is theological and involves a spiritual recrudescence and improvement of human character that will synchronize with our almost matchless advances in science, art, literature, and with all materials and cultural developments of the past 2,000 years. It must be of the spirit if we are to save the flesh! (*Reminiscences*, McGraw Hill, p. 88)

God's method of changing human character is through imparting a new nature, but because man has rejected the Gospel, we move ever closer to Armageddon. MacArthur's message nevertheless communicates a vital truth: there is a limit to what man can do with military hardware to insure survival. Wise Solomon agreed: "The horse is prepared against the day of battle: but safety is of the Lord" (Prov. 21:31).

There may not be a point of safety at which our nation can arrive in the area of defense. No amount of expenditure for weaponry can assure survival. But America need not fall, especially if we are willing to fall on our knees. God's protection is not limited by a lack of sufficient firepower.

The Bible is rich in examples of deliverance and victory for the underarmed and undermanned. Has God's power diminished since the days of Joshua, Gideon, and David?

When considering the sufficiency of military power for the safety of his nation, the psalmist cried: "Some trust in chariots, and some in horses: but we will remember the name of the Lord our God" (Ps. 20:7). Is this kind of confidence out of date? Or is our faith weak?

In his challenging book, *The Root of the Righteous*, A. W. Tozer wrote of "pseudo faith." He explained:

We can prove our faith by our committal to it and in no other way. Any belief that does not command the one who holds it is not a real belief; it is a pseudo belief only. And it might shock some of us profoundly if we were brought suddenly face to face with our beliefs and forced to test them in the fires of practical living.

Many of us Christians have become extremely skillful in arranging our lives so as to admit the truth of Christianity without being embarrassed by its implications. We arrange things so that we can get on well enough without divine aid, while at the same time ostensibly seeking it. We boast in the Lord but watch carefully that we never get caught depending on Him.

Pseudo faith always arranges a way out to serve in case God fails it. Real faith knows only one way and gladly allows itself to be stripped of any second way or makeshift substitutes. For true faith, it is either God or total collapse. And not since Adam first stood up on earth has God failed a single man or woman who trusted Him (Christian Publications, pp. 49-50).

This is not to say that supporting a national defense program is contrary to faith. God watched over and gave victories to the armies of Joshua, Gideon, and David. But the victories came as the leaders and their people walked in faith. Can we still identify with Gideon as he saw his thousands depart, leaving him with a force of only 300 men with whom to defeat the Midianites? (Judges 7:6) Would we have dared go along with Joshua's strategy for conquering Jericho because God had revealed that the city would fall miraculously to the Israelites as a result of faith and obedience? (Joshua 6) Where are the Christian leaders who will remind the church that prayer power is more important than firepower?

Perhaps now more than ever, believers must be careful not to be awed and influenced by the statements of politicians and military men. We are in danger of being too impressed by their knowledge of world affairs or modern weaponry.

Power is persuasive. None of us is immune from being overwhelmed by the sheer force of the personalities of important people. We should remember that the track records of kings and generals are not all that good and the future of this world's leaders is not all that promising. The Apostle John wrote,

And I saw an angel standing in the sun; and he cried with a loud voice, saying to all the fowls that fly in the midst of heaven, "Come and gather yourselves together unto the supper of the great God: that ye may eat the flesh of kings, and the flesh of captains, and the flesh of mighty men, and the flesh of horses, and of them that sit on them, and the flesh of all men, both free and bond, both small and great" (Rev. 19:17-18).

Confidence in the destructiveness and accuracy of modern weaponry may be a significant sign of the end. The

Antichrist will call the heads of the various parts of his empire to assemble their armies for the Battle of Armageddon. These end time political leaders, under the direction of the final world dictator, will then gather their forces in the Middle East to destroy Christ when He returns: "And I saw the beast, and the kings of the earth, and their armies, gathered together to make war against Him that sat on the horse, and against His army" (Rev. 19:19).

This military venture will fail. Our Lord will victoriously end the Battle of Armageddon before establishing His earthly kingdom, demonstrating to all the world that He is greater than any weapon produced by man.

But today the world desperately needs Christians who call others to trust in God's protection. When Robert Bruce, the famous emancipator of Scotland, fled from his enemies, he sought refuge in a cave. By the time his pursuers reached his hideout a spider had spun a web over the mouth of the cave, so they concluded that he could not have hidden there. Bruce prayed, "O God, I thank Thee that in the tiny bowels of a spider You can place for me a shelter, and then send the spider in time to place it for my protection" (Walter B. Knight, *Knight's Master Book of New Illustrations*, Eerdmans, pp. 531-532).

God may choose to protect us as He has others in troubled times. Who can say how much power is generated by millions of praying Christians? Let us not be diverted from the way of faith, lest we miss God's great alternative route to survival.

6 THE GATES OF HELL

Twentieth-century Christians are not the first to live in tense times. The church was born in adversity and on a collision course with the world. There were no nuclear weapons in the first century, but one is as dead after a stoning, a crucifixion, or beheading as after a nuclear blast.

The Lord warned His disciples of coming persecutions—preaching the Gospel in a sinful world carries built-in hazards. Jesus Himself was the object of attack by those who were convicted by His righteous life and clear message, and He told His followers to expect the same. "If the world hate you, ye know that it hated Me before it hated you. If ye were of the world, the world would love its own; but because ye are not of the world, but I have chosen you out of the world, therefore the world hateth you. Remember the word that I said unto you, 'The servant is not greater than his lord.' If they have persecuted Me, they will also persecute you; if they have kept My saying, they will keep yours also" (John 15:18-20).

This early warning was on target.

The church has suffered through the centuries.

On returning from a field of service, a missionary once said, "If someone had sent me on a journey and told me the road to take, warning me that at a certain point I would come to a dangerous crossing of a river, at another point to a forest infested with wild beasts, I would face those dangers with the satisfaction of knowing I was on the right road" (Walter B. Knight, *Three Thousand Illustrations for Christian Service*, Eerdmans, p. 492).

While the Lord prophesied persecutions, He also guaranteed the survival of His church: "And I say also unto thee, 'That thou art Peter, and upon this rock I will build My church; and the gates of hell shall not prevail against it' " (Matt. 16:18).

The history of the church reveals the accuracy of our Lord's prophecy. A flood of opposition and vicious persecution battered the church from its beginning. The odds against its survival seemed insurmountable, but the church exists today, a witness to God's loving care and His sovereignty.

Becoming a Christian in New Testament times was hazardous. On Pentecost, 3,000 Jews who had come to Jerusalem that day were converted to Christ and baptized. Their joy was unbounded as they experienced forgiveness, knew the presence of the indwelling Holy Spirit, broke bread with the disciples, and began to learn the doctrines of the faith. But difficult days were ahead.

Peter and John

Peter and John invited trouble with the priests and the Sadducees in Jerusalem because through them a lame beggar was healed. Rather than being pleased at this demonstration of God's power, the religious leaders grieved over the enthusiasm of the people's response to the disciples' message of the death and resurrection of Christ, by whose power the man had been made whole. By nightfall, they had imprisoned Peter and John (Acts 3—4:4).

Stephen

Stephen's preaching against the sins of his hearers so enraged them that they rushed him out of the city and ended his life with a barrage of stones. Stephen spent his final moments praying for his executioners, setting an example for other martyrs of the faith in the centuries to follow.

Christ's Love for His Followers

In the story of Stephen's martyrdom is a moving illustration of Christ's compassion for His own in their trials. Just before his death, Stephen was given a glimpse of heaven where he saw Jesus standing on the right hand of God (Acts 7:55-56). Of this experience, Dr. H. A. Ironside wrote:

> Here is a very significant thing. We are told in the Epistle to the Hebrews that when Jesus had by Himself purged our sins, He sat down on the right hand of the Majesty on high; and here, as Stephen looked up, he saw the Lord standing. What does it mean? It is just as though the blessed Lord in His great compassion for Stephen has risen from His seat and is looking over the battlements of heaven to strengthen and cheer the martyr down on earth" (*Lectures on Acts*, Loizeaux, pp. 174-175).

The Lord's tender care for His persecuted people is also demonstrated at the conversion of Saul of Tarsus, who zealously persecuted the early believers. At the time of his conversion, he was traveling to Damascus with letters from the high priest in Jerusalem giving him permission to pursue his deadly work.

As he traveled, a light from heaven suddenly surrounded him. He fell to the earth and heard a voice saying, "Saul, Saul, why persecutest thou Me?" (Acts 9:4) Saul had never physically laid a hand on Jesus, but our Lord was so identified with believers that in persecuting them, Saul was persecuting Jesus.

Peter, Paul, and Others

Saul was converted but persecution continued. Others more violent stepped up the attack on the church. Herod killed James. He imprisoned Peter, but the church went to prayer and Peter was miraculously delivered on the eve of his execution (Acts 12:3-17). God was at work, making good His guarantee of the church's survival.

Paul and Silas were beaten and imprisoned, with their feet placed in stocks, but they were set free at midnight by an earthquake that caused the prison doors to open and their chains to fall off (Acts 16:22-26). At Corinth, Paul's life was in jeopardy when opposition to his preaching arose, but his safety was certified by the Lord Himself: "Then spake the Lord to Paul in the night by a vision, 'Be not afraid, but speak, and hold not thy peace: for I am with thee, and no man shall set on thee: for I have much people in this city' " (Acts 18:9-10). Paul remained safely in Corinth for six more months teaching the Word of God to the believers. He was the safest man in the city.

When Paul preached in Jerusalem, he caused such an uproar that the chief military officer feared the mob might literally pull Paul apart. There was no need for alarm. If Paul had any personal fears, they were calmed by a special revelation of his mission. "And the night following the Lord stood by him, and said, 'Be of good cheer, Paul, for as thou hast testified of Me in Jerusalem, so must thou bear witness also at Rome' " (Acts 23:11).

From that time on there was no doubt about Paul's survival of the trip between Jerusalem and Rome. Come plot or shipwreck, Paul would make it through. Paul, being human, evidently needed some encouragement during a storm at sea, and so it was given: "Fear not, Paul; thou must be brought before Caesar: and lo, God hath given thee all them that sail with thee" (Acts 27:24).

God graciously allows for our frailty but His purposes are sure to be fulfilled. We may rest in this truth rather than being shaken by the panic peddlers of our day.

Polycarp

Persecution of believers continued after the Apostolic Age. Nero's atrocities have already been described. Other emperors were equally as fierce in their assault on the church.

Outstanding among the martyrs in the early centuries was Polycarp of Smyrna. Polycarp, who had been taught by the apostles, was arrested and brought into the amphitheater in Smyrna. The proconsul promised to release him if he would turn from his belief. Guaranteeing his destiny, Polycarp answered, "Eighty and six years I have served Him, and He has never done me wrong; how can I blaspheme Him, my King, who has saved me? I am a Christian."

To the crowd the proconsul proclaimed, "Polycarp has confessed himself to be a Christian!"

The crowd yelled, "Let him be burned!"

As he stood on his grave of wood, Polycarp asked not to be nailed to the stake. "Leave me thus," he said. "He who strengthens me to endure the flames will also enable me to stand firm at the stake without being fastened with nails."

As the flames grew hot, Polycarp prayed loudly, "Lord God Almighty, Father of our Lord Jesus Christ, I praise Thee that Thou has judged me worthy of this day and of this hour, to participate in the number of Thy witnesses, and in the cup of Thy Christ (B. K. Kuiper, *The Church in History*, National Union of Christian Schools and Eerdmans, pp. 9-10).

An untold number of Christians were executed when the emperor Marcus Aurelius (A.D. 161-180) decreed that the property of Christians should be given to their accusers. The results were predictable (Kuiper, *The Church*, p. 10).

John Wesley

John Wesley once preached at an outdoor meeting where the crowd became hostile. Wesley said later:

Many of the people acted like beasts and did their best to disturb the meeting. They tried to drive a herd of cows into the crowd, but without success. Then they began to throw stones—showers of them. One of them struck me between the eyes. I wiped away the blood, and went right on, declaring that God has given to them that believe, 'not the spirit of fear, but of power, and of love, and of a sound mind.' By the spirit which now appeared ... I saw what a blessing it is when it is given us, even in the lowest degree to suffer for His name's sake!" (Walter Knight, *Knight's Treasury of Illustrations*, Eerdmans, p. 261)

Nonviolent Attacks

Not all of the attacks against the church are physical. The enemy has often come as an angel of light, causing divisions and strife between believers. Even the early church was not immune from schisms that hindered the work of Christ. The church at Corinth was torn by infighting and weakened by carnality and immorality. The Galatian church was confused by false teaching about law and grace when legalizers perverted the truth.

Nevertheless, the church has endured. In dangerous times and trying situations believers have stood firm and faithful, even when it meant martyrdom.

How did the early church survive under such pressures? Believers kept in mind the encouragement of Paul and Peter:

For I reckon that the sufferings of this present time are not worthy to be compared with the glory which shall be revealed in us (Rom. 8:18). Beloved, think it not strange concerning the fiery trial which is to try you, as though some strange thing happened unto you: But rejoice, inasmuch as ye are partakers of Christ's sufferings; that, when His glory shall be revealed, ye may be glad also with exceeding joy (1 Peter 4:12-13).

What can we learn from the first-century Christians that will enable us to survive in these perilous times?

7 THE WORLD UPSETTERS

After Christ's ascension 120 believers, newly commissioned to take the Gospel to the entire world, met to pray in an Upper Room in Jerusalem. Still fresh in their minds was the charge of their Lord: "But ye shall receive power after that the Holy Ghost is come upon you, and ye shall be witnesses unto Me both in Jerusalem, and in all Judea, and in Samaria, and unto the uttermost part of the earth" (Acts 1:8).

The task must have seemed impossible. There were plenty of reasons to expect the worst. Peter, soon to be their chief spokesman, had recently denied his Lord three times and had been heard cursing and swearing. Women in the group had doubted the Lord's promise that He would rise from the grave and had come to the tomb with spices to do the work of undertakers (Luke 24:1). After the resurrection, Thomas couldn't muster enough faith to believe it had actually taken place. Now the greatest shame was one of their reasons for meeting: Judas had betrayed Jesus, and they must choose another man to take his place. Their survival as a group, let alone any success in their mission, must have seemed doubtful.

But 10 days later all was changed.

On the Day of Pentecost, 3,000 Jews who had assembled in Jerusalem were converted to Christ through the witnessing and preaching of those who had met in the Upper Room. Not long after that they had gained the reputation of upsetters of the world (Acts 17:6).

Those first-century Christians should be an example to us. They triumphed while living in the most difficult conditions. They had none of our modern tools for evangelism or aids to worship, but they were far more effective in fulfilling the Lord's commission than we are today. Without printing presses, parachurch organizations, radio and television ministries, or even church buildings, they effectively planted the church all over the then-known world. By the end of the first century A.D., their number had increased from 120 to approximately 10 million. The church exists throughout the world today because that unlikely company was faithful.

The Secret of Their Power

The early Christians simply obeyed orders, held to the basics, and conquered.

A minister came to see me because a cloud of depression seemed to hover continually over him. He wondered if life was worth living and had asked the Lord many times to end his earthly life and take him to heaven. In his search for answers, my friend had attended a number of "deeper life" conferences, making a point to have a session alone with the speakers in the hope of gleaning the secret of personal victory.

I wondered whether I could tell this defeated preacher something he had not already heard. Then, almost surprised at my own action, I handed him a Gospel of John.

"Think of yourself as a new Christian," I advised. "You may need to return to the basics."

My "treatment" for this troubled servant of God was correct. Later I heard him sharing his new found victory with other ministers and telling them how it had come about. What the supposed "spiritual secrets" could not do was accomplished through a return to the simple message of Christ and His love.

First-century Christians survived and were successful because they did not major on minors. Their task was clear: to preach the Gospel to every creature. They made this task their principle occupation.

Early believers were often in danger of imprisonment or death because of their faith and message, but they were so committed to their mission that courage came naturally. They prayed and moved ahead regardless of the consequences: "And when they had prayed, the place was shaken where they were assembled together; and they were all filled with the Holy Ghost, and they spake the Word of God with boldness" (Acts 4:31).

When religious or governmental authorities tried to stop them, these bold believers replied that they were compelled to obey God rather than men. Execution seemed to be the only way to silence them, but when their enemies took that route, the church flourished more than ever. The Christians served under a higher authority than any on earth and they did not hesitate to say so: "But Peter and John answered and said unto them, 'Whether it be right in the sight of God to hearken unto you more than unto God, judge ye. For we cannot but speak the things which we have seen and heard'" (Acts 4:19-20).

"Weaknesses" of the Church
In some areas, the New Testament church was powerless.

It was without financial power. One of Peter's first pronouncements revealed the poverty of the church: "Then

Peter said, 'Silver and gold have I none; but such as I have give I thee: In the name of Jesus Christ of Nazareth rise up and walk' " (Acts 3:6).

If the early church had waited to evangelize the world till it was financially sound, the task would never have been started. Those first believers had to sell their belongings and pool their resources just to survive: "And all that believed were together, and had all things common; and sold their possessions and goods and parted them to all men, as every man had need" (Acts 2:44-45).

Some view this sharing of belongings as an experiment in Christian communism, but it was, rather, a collective act of love among brothers and sisters in Christ who needed to solve an immediate problem. Believers, many of whom were far from home, numbered in the thousands. In order to provide the necessities for this growing multitude, local converts and those from other areas who had possessions with them sold these belongings to make it possible for all to live.

Note the difference between New Testament practice and the philosophy of present-day survivalists. In the early church, the believers gave freely of what they had to provide enough for all. There was no holding back among those who were genuine in their faith. The exception to this common sacrifice is found in only one couple, Ananias and Sapphira, who considered their personal survival more important than that of the other believers. Their lying about the amount they had received from the sale of their property cost them their lives (Acts 5:1-11).

The church was also without political power. The apostles could not pull strings in high places, and there is no evidence that these courageous souls ever sought influence among the powerful of their world.

Paul was frequently brought before government officials

but did not seek to exert influence over them. Instead, he was concerned for their souls. When he was brought before the chief military officer in Jerusalem, Paul recounted his conversion to Christ in great detail, confessing his persecution of believers and testifying to the change that had taken place in his life.

Before Governor Felix, Paul stressed the truth of the Resurrection and evidently became quite personal in his effort to persuade the governor of his need of salvation. The writer of Acts says of Felix's reaction: "And as [Paul] reasoned of righteousness, temperance, and judgment to come, Felix trembled, and answered, 'Go thy way for this time; when I have a convenient season, I will call for thee' " (Acts 24:25).

Standing before King Agrippa, Paul seized another opportunity to tell of his conversion and of God's work in his life. So effective was the apostle's witness that the king said, "Almost thou persuadest me to be a Christian" (Acts 26:28).

Paul was powerful in witnessing, but he knew no one in Jerusalem or Rome who could help the church or even reverse the charges brought unjustly against him.

Political impotence had not always been Paul's lot. Before his conversion, he had enjoyed influence with both political and religious leaders. But after his conversion, he was, like other believers, part of a peculiar group given to evangelizing the world without regard for prestige offered by the world.

The survival and triumph of that first body of adherents to the Christian faith is nothing short of a miracle. It can be explained only by recognizing that the church possessed power that transcended and exceeded the financial, political, and social power that was marshaled against it.

A. W. Tozer observed:

It was not an easy task which the church faced when she came down from that Upper Room. To carry on the work of a Man who was known to have died—to have died as criminals die—and more than that, to persuade others that this Man had risen again from the dead and that He was the Son of God and Saviour: this mission was, in the nature of it, doomed to failure from the start. Who would credit such a fantastic story? Who would put faith in One whom society had condemned and crucified? Left to herself the church must have perished as a thousand abortive sects had done before her, and have nothing for a future generation to remember.

That the church did not so perish was due entirely to the miraculous element within her. That element was supplied by the Holy Spirit who came at Pentecost to empower her for her task. For the church was not an organization merely, not a movement, but a walking incarnation of spiritual energy. And she accomplished within a few brief years such prodigies of moral conquest as to leave us wholly without an explanation—apart from God.

In short, the church began in power, moved in power, and moved just as long as she had power (*Paths to Power*, Christian Publications, pp. 3-4).

Few would question Tozer's conclusion. The early Christians moved in power that could not be slowed even by the most hideous of persecutions. Wherever the messengers and the message went, power was present. Multitudes believed. Lives were changed. Churches were established. The moral and spiritual lives of whole communities were affected.

The Power of the Church Today

Now we must face a sobering question: Does the church today possess the same power as the early church? Power is vital, as Tozer further said,

If we are to advance we must have power. Paganism is slowly closing in on the church, and her only response is an occasional "drive" for one thing or another—usually money—or a noisy but timid campaign to improve the morals of the movies. Such activities amount to little more than a slight twitching of the muscles of a drowsy giant too sleepy to care. These efforts sometimes reach the headlines, but they accomplish little that is lasting, and are soon forgotten. The church must have power; she must become formidable, a moral force to be reckoned with, if she would regain her lost position of spiritual ascendance and make her message the revolutionizing, conquering thing it once was (*Paths*, pp. 4-5).

If the church seems to lack the power of God, the temptation is to use other power sources. The church of Laodicea had substituted the power of money for the power of God and was rebuked for it in John's prophecy: "I know thy works, that thou art neither cold nor hot. I would thou wert cold or hot. So then because thou art neither cold nor hot, I will spew thee out of My mouth. Because thou sayest, I am rich, and increased with goods, and have need of nothing; and knowest not that thou art wretched, and miserable, and poor, and blind, and naked. I counsel thee to buy of Me gold tried in the fire that thou mayest be rich" (Rev. 3:15-18).

A church that cannot influence the community through evangelism, righteous living, and members' individual involvement in good government may be tempted to substitute political power for the power of God.

There is a better way. The power of God that flowed through His people in the first century is still available today. God has not changed. The Great Commission has not changed. The power of the Holy Spirit has not diminished.

It is time to revive the church into the world-upsetting force it once was, for revival may be the key to survival for believers in the trying times ahead.

8 REVIVAL: KEY TO SURVIVAL?

In the United States, we may think of a revival as a series of spring or fall meetings conducted by a visiting speaker or musical group and limited in effect to one local church. The success or failure of the effort may be measured by the evangelist's appeal to the congregation, the size of the crowds attending the meetings, or the amount of the love offering.

Definitions of Revival

Walter Boldt, a man active in a recent Canadian awakening, says revival is "God at work, restoring His church to health." Another Canadian observer sees revival as "the inrush of the Spirit into a body that threatens to become a corpse." The great English evangelist Jonathan Goforth said, "Revival is simply the Spirit of God fully controlling the surrendered life" (Erwin W. Lutzer, *Flames of Freedom*, Moody Press, pp. 136-137).

Charles G. Finny, great American revivalist of the 19th century, explained revival as "the renewal of the first love of Christians, resulting in the awakening and conversion of sinners to God. [It] is nothing else than a new beginning of obedience to God" (*Revivals of Religion*, Moody Press, pp. 14-15).

David C. Enger, writing in the *Radio Bible Class Discovery Digest*, defines revival as "a spontaneous spiritual awakening produced by the Holy Spirit." He says this awakening results in a deepened sensitivity to God and His Word, a holy walk produced by a heightened awareness of sin, and a renewed concern for lost souls (p. 8).

William B. Sprague said revival occurs "Wherever you see religion rising up from a state of comparative depression to a tone of increased vigor and strength; wherever you see professing Christians becoming more faithful to their obligations, and behold the strength of the church increased by fresh accessions of piety; there is a state of things which you need not hesitate to denominate as a revival of religion" (quoted by Stephen Olford, *Heart Cry for Revival*, Revell, p. 15).

In his book *In the Day of Thy Power*, Arthur Wallis writes, The meaning of any word is determined by its usage. For a definition of revival we must therefore appeal to the people of God of bygone years, who have used the word with consistency of meaning down through the centuries, until it came to be used in a lesser and more limited sense in modern times. Numerous writings on the subject that have been preserved to us will confirm that revival is divine intervention in the normal course of spiritual things. It is God revealing Himself to man in awful holiness and irresistible power. It is such a manifest working of God that human personalities are overshadowed, and human programs abandoned. It is man retiring into the background because God has taken the field. It is the Lord making bare His holy arm, and working in extraordinary power on saint and sinner (quoted in *Heart Cry for Revival*, p. 16).

Stephen Olford concludes that:

Revival is that strange and sovereign work of God in which He visits His own people, restoring, reanimating, and releasing them into the fullness of His blessing. Such a divine intervention will issue in evangelism though, in the first instance, it is a work of God in the church and amongst individual believers. Once we understand the nature of heaven-sent revival, we shall be able to think, pray, and speak intelligently of such "times of refreshing . . . from the presence of the Lord" (Acts 3:19) (*Heart Cry*, p. 17).

In the Old Testament, revival prayers were calls for God to restore Israel to the place of righteousness, blessing, prosperity, freedom, and spiritual power they had known before. The psalmist cried, "Wilt Thou not revive us again: that Thy people may rejoice in Thee?" (Ps. 85:6) The Prophet Habakkuk said, "O Lord, I have heard Thy speech, and was afraid. O Lord, revive Thy work in the midst of the years, in the midst of the years remember mercy" (3:2).

Today, revival in a church is a return to the power, love, righteousness and outreach called for by the Lord in His letter to the church at Ephesus: "Remember therefore from whence thou art fallen, and repent, and do the first works" (Rev. 2:5).

The church has strayed. God has not moved. It is time to return.

Revival of Love

A Colombian became a Christian through studying the Bible and soon immigrated to the United States. He searched for a church in which he could learn more about his newfound faith, but became confused by the great number of denominations. He finally decided on a test for choosing a church to which he could belong. He would know he had found the right one when he saw the love of Christ as evident as it was in the New Testament church.

This new Christian's criterion may not satisfy everyone—other fundamentals also need to be considered. Nevertheless, I am challenged every time I think of this new convert's keen perception of the climate of the early church. A return of that climate always accompanies revival. Old hurts are laid aside. Forgiveness flows freely. Malice is put away.

Writing of conditions during the Great Awakening, the English preacher Jonathan Edwards said: "Our converts, then, remarkably appeared united in dear affection to one another, and many have expressed much of that spirit of love which they felt toward all mankind; and particularly to those who had been least friendly to them. Never, I believe, was so much done in confessing injuries, and making up differences as the last year" (*The Narrative*, Kregel Publications, p. 70).

Revival of Unity

A return to New Testament love would, by its very nature, provoke a return to the unity of the early church. This does not mean that union is to be achieved by removing denominational barriers or sacrificing convictions. Rather, unity is to exist in local congregations as it did between the disciples in the Upper Room and the converts after Pentecost. The Book of Acts describes this single-mindedness: "These all continued with one accord in prayer and supplication, with the women, and Mary the mother of Jesus, and with His brethren" (1:14). "And they, continuing daily with one accord in the temple, and breaking bread from house to house, did eat their meat with gladness and singleness of heart" (2:46).

Contrast this warm, cooperative attitude with the tense atmosphere in many churches today and it is not difficult to understand the church's ineffectiveness. We are not world-upsetters; we are church-upsetters.

The carnality so evident in the Corinthian church (1 Cor. 3:3) is now epidemic. Our easy way of life fosters the self-centeredness that causes so much factionalism. Energy and time that we could give to prayer, spiritual growth, and outreach are instead used to keep the flock from scattering and the church from falling apart.

The victims of the little groups that divide are often the pastors, who leave depressed and ineffective. During a speaking engagement in a metropolitan church, I was approached by a couple who shocked me with their blunt statement: "We'd like to have revival here, but we're afraid if we do, the pastor will be encouraged, and stay." Revival did not come to that church and the pastor did not stay.

Revival of Separation

A genuine revival would also call for a return to New Testament separation. The apostles drew a clear line between temporal and eternal things and made it clear which the church should choose. Those early believers were reminded that they were citizens of heaven (Phil. 3:20) who, though surrounded on every hand by opportunities and entice-ments, were to set their hearts on things above (Col. 3:2).

Sometimes Christians have interpreted separation from the world to mean only that one must abstain from partici-pation in a half-dozen different practices. That concept not only misses the point, but it also omits too many things that are worldly.

But what is the world?

John Wesley said, "Whatever cools my affection toward Christ is the world." J. Wilbur Chapman further said, "Any-thing that dims my vision of Christ, or takes away my taste for Bible study, or cramps my prayer life, or makes Christian work more difficult, is wrong for me and I must, as a Christian, turn away from it" (Walter B. Knight, *Knight's Treasury of Illustrations*, Eerdmans, p. 443).

We are to be separated from the world, but it is equally important to be separated *unto God*. Those who focus on dedication to Christ will have little trouble in allowing the old life to fade out of the picture. The early Christians discovered it was not legalism but love for Christ and one another that made their lives dynamic and their witness effective.

Revival, then, produces a fresh emphasis on holy living—it is characteristic of every great spiritual awakening. Religious stirrings that do not result in righteousness in daily living are counterfeit.

Revival of Evangelism

Revival cannot be divorced from evangelism. The work of God that awakens believers to sin also creates compassion for sinners. Jonathan Edwards said of the Great Awakening: "Persons after their own conversion have commonly expressed an exceedingly great desire for the conversion of others. Some have thought that they should be willing to die for the conversion of any soul, though, of one of the meanest of their fellow creatures, or of one of their worst enemies. And many have indeed been in great distress with desires and longings for it" (*The Narrative*, p. 70).

If we are to survive, there must be a return to the fiery evangelism of New Testament times. Outreach at home and abroad must be the aim of every believer's existence.

Explaining that evangelism is a natural result of revival, Charles Finney said,

Christians will have their faith renewed. While they are in their backslidden state they are blind to the state of sinners. Their hearts are as hard as marble. The truths of the Bible only appear like a dream. They admit it to be all true, their conscience and their judgment assent to it; but their faith does not see it standing out in bold relief, in all the burning realities of eternity. But when they enter into a revival, they no longer see men as trees walking, but they see things in that strong light which will renew the love of God in their hearts. This will lead them to labor zealously to bring others to Him. They will feel grieved that others do not love God, when they love Him so much. And they will set themselves feelingly to persuade their neighbors to give Him their hearts. So their love to men will be renewed. They will be filled with a tender, burning love for souls. They will have a longing desire for the salvation of the whole world (*Revivals*, pp. 15-16).

But what has happened in our churches? The machinery works, but we advance at a snail's pace. We have lost the evangelistic fire that propelled the early church across the world preaching the Gospel and planting churches.

What is the remedy? Revival. But what if revival comes? What if we return to the love and unity of the early church? What if we embrace holiness and evangelism with the same dedication and fire of first-century believers?

Does Revival Mean Survival?

Is there any biblical support for the teaching that revival may indeed save our land?

Several cases seem to support the idea that a turning to God can save people and even cities from destruction. Had there been 10 righteous people in Sodom, it would have been spared the fires of judgment (Gen. 18:32). Nineveh was 40 days away from doom when Jonah began to call the people to repentance, and this sin city was spared when the people repented and turned to God (Jonah 3).

God promised His people: "If My people, which are called

by My name, shall humble themselves, and pray, and seek My face, and turn from their wicked ways; then will I hear from heaven, and will forgive their sin and will heal their land" (2 Chron. 7:14). If we knew that God would heal our land if we met the conditions of revival, would we meet them?

The situation is serious. There is no place to hide. Political leaders grope for answers. Advances in modern technology only seem to move us closer to doomsday.

In other times of crisis, God has delivered His people and enabled them to survive when they have sought Him with all their hearts.

Can it happen now?

9 GREAT REVIVALS OF THE PAST

The church was born in revival. On the Day of Pentecost a discouraged group of believers became a dynamic witnessing force. It was an unlikely event, but at the end of the day, 3,000 had been added to the church at Jerusalem.

Commenting on this miracle, Dr. John R. Rice wrote:

Let that defeated, unreliable, immature bunch of disciples reassemble and try to have a revival now in Jerusalem! Let Peter, who cursed so loudly a few weeks ago and denied that he even knew Jesus, now try to preach Christ to these multitudes! What chance have they for a revival in Jerusalem?

But they had it nevertheless! They waited in an Upper Room for 10 days. "These all continued with one accord in prayer and supplication, with the women, and Mary the mother of Jesus, and with His brethren" (Acts 1:14). And when the Day of Pentecost was fully come, the power of God came upon them. They were filled with the Holy Spirit as John had been filled, as Jesus had been filled at His baptism. They were filled with the Holy Spirit, and they spoke the Word of God with boldness and power. God stretched out His hand to give miraculous confirmation of their message. Sinners were cut to the heart, there was a great repenting, and 3,000 people were saved in one day and added to the church! Then multitudes of others were saved day after day, in the mighty initial revival, the sample revival which God gave early in the age for all of us to know what He could do and wanted to do in revivals (*We Can Have Revival Now*, Sword of the Lord, p. 92).

The revival on the Day of Pentecost followed the pattern of all true revivals. Believers put away their differences. They prayerfully surrendered themselves to God and were ready to be filled when the Holy Spirit came in fulfillment of the promise of Christ: "Nevertheless I tell you the truth: It is expedient for you that I go away: for if I go not away, the Comforter will not come unto you; but if I depart, I will send Him unto you" (John 16:7). "But ye shall receive power, after that the Holy Ghost is come upon you: and ye shall be witnesses unto Me both in Jerusalem and in all Judea, and in Samaria, and unto the uttermost part of the earth" (Acts 1:8).

But the Holy Spirit did not come on the Day of Pentecost because a revival had broken out. Dr. H. A. Ironside cautioned: "Do not make a mistake. Pentecost did not come because they were of single unity and in one place; they were there expecting Pentecost, in obedience to the words of the Lord Jesus Christ. Pentecost was a predetermined epoch in the mind of God and the Word of God. It had been settled from all past ages just when the Holy Spirit was to descend and take up His abode with the people of God on earth" (*Lectures on Acts*, Loizeaux Brothers, p. 39).

Having said that, however, it is important to realize that though the Holy Spirit indwelt and empowered the disciples as had been promised, their yielded wills provided clear channels through which the power of God could produce the revival.

The disciples could have quenched the Spirit (1 Thes. 5:19). They didn't, and the revival came. "When they had prayed, the place was shaken where they were assembled together; and they were all filled with the Holy Ghost, and they spake the Word of God with boldness.... And with great power gave the apostles witness of the Lord Jesus: and great grace was upon them all" (Acts 4:31, 33).

The Book of Acts tells the stories of repeated revivals because it chronicles the lives of Spirit-filled people. It is only when *we* yield completely to the Holy Spirit that personal revival comes, and conversely, revival does not come if we are not yielded to Him. In his book, *More Power to the Church*, David M. Dawson explained:

One of the most tragic statements of the Gospels is that Jesus Christ was in the world, and the world was made by Him, and the world knew Him not.

When the light of eternity is flashed on our day, one of the most tragic truths that we shall see revealed will be that the Holy Spirit was in the church in our day, and He made the church, and the church knew Him not.

A sweeping revival would come to Protestantism if Christian workers of the world would realize that all real success in Christian work is dependent on our relationship with the Holy Spirit. Power is God, the Holy Spirit, at work in us and through us (Zondervan, pp. 12, 15).

Though historians have not recorded many revivals of the past, surely unnumbered times of refreshing have come to individuals and local congregations, lifting them from despair to heights of blessing. Barriers between Christians have been broken down. Christian love has replaced cold indifference and hypocrisy. Prayer has intensified; faith increased. The joy of the Lord has become a part of worship. Evangelism has flourished.

Some revivals could not be contained in one community but spread like wildfire, changing lives, awakening churches, and influencing nations. These times of refreshing have been recorded for us, and some of them will now become the subject of our study. Perhaps our exposure to these will light some fires within us and cause the holy flames to spread once more.

The Great Awakening

As the 18th century dawned, America was in a sad spiritual condition. The founders of the New England colonies had been people of strong Christian conviction. Their grandchildren, however, had settled down to lukewarm religion or had completely departed from the faith, taken in by the deism and rationalism sweeping across Europe and England, and finally America. Religious fervor was almost non-existent. Morality was in swift decline. There was little evidence of genuine Christianity.

In 1727, 24-year-old Jonathan Edwards, a recent graduate of Yale College, was called to assist his grandfather, the pastor of the Congregational Church of Northampton, Massachusetts. Two years after his move to Northampton, the grandfather died and young Edwards became the pastor of one of the largest, wealthiest, and most cultured congregations in New England.

It is not likely that this congregation expected their young pastor to be the key personality in a great spiritual awakening, but with real Christianity at low ebb, Jonathan Edwards gave himself to earnest prayer for revival. In 1735 the fire fell at his Congregational church and spread to all of New England and beyond. The work of God in the church had an almost immediate effect on the surrounding area. Jonathan Edwards described what happened:

There scarcely was a single person in the town, old or young, left unconcerned about the great things of the eternal world. Those who were wont to be the vainest and loosest, and those who had been most disposed to think and speak lightly of vital and experiential religion, were now generally subject to great awakenings. And the work of conversion was carried on in a most astonishing manner and increased more and more; souls did come, as it were, by flocks to Jesus Christ. From day to day, for many months together, might be seen evident instances of sinners brought out of darkness into marvelous light and delivered out of a horrible pit, and from the miry clay, and set upon a rock, with a new song of praise to God in their mouths (Ps. 40:1-3).

This work of God, as it was carried on, and the number of true saints multiplied, soon made a glorious alteration in the town; so that in the spring and summer following, and 1735, the town seemed to be full of the presence of God: it never was so full of love, nor of joy, and yet so full of distress, as it was then. There were remarkable tokens of God's presence in almost every house. It was a time of joy in families on account of salvation being brought unto them; parents rejoicing over their children as newborn, and husbands over their wives and wives over their husbands. The goings of God were then seen in His sanctuary, God's day was a delight, and His tabernacles were amiable. Our public assemblies were then beautiful: the congregation was alive in God's service, everyone earnestly intent upon the public worship, every hearer eager to drink in the words of the minister as they came from his mouth; the assembly in general were, from time to time, in tears while the Word was preached; some weeping with sorrow and distress, others with joy and love, others with pity and concern for the souls of their neighbors (*The Narrative*, Kregel Publications, pp. 25-26).

The fire spread from town to town and from county to county. By 1740 all of New England was alive with revival. Many were converted to Christ. The moral tone of New England was lifted. Between 25,000 and 50,000 new members were added to the churches.

At this same time, missionary David Brainerd saw a remarkable awakening among the Indians. Brainerd had labored long and hard with few results, but now those who had been cold to his message were eager to hear him. Sometimes they came streaming in on him, pressing about him, grasping the bridle of his horse, and asking the way of salvation.

The Great Awakening also reached England, where the Wesleys were laboring to bring revival. Their contemporary, George Whitefield, one of the most eloquent preachers in the recent history of the church, made an important contribution to the revivals taking place on both sides of the Atlantic.

James A. Stewart made a significant observation concerning The Great Awakening. He pointed out that it began in the ordinary course of a faithful pastor's ministry, adding: "The blessing was not the outcome of a well-organized and highly-advertised evangelistic effort. It was a supernatural work of God in spontaneous awakening, in answer to the prayers of the godly leader of the flock. This was a *revival* in the scriptural sense of the word, for the true spirit of revival eludes the grasp of the organizer and the advertiser. It cannot be created by machinery nor promoted by printer's ink" (*The Narrative*, p. 21).

What an encouraging thought! Revival lies within the reach of any pastor and flock. A great awakening awaits any congregation that longs for it and is willing to pay revival's price.

The Wesleyan Revival

John Wesley's life (1703-1791) spanned nearly the entire 18th century. He was God's man of the hour for England.

In the early part of the century, social and moral conditions in England were deplorable. Coarseness and brutality were characteristics of the time. Public amusements were designed to appeal to the lowest in man. Drunkenness was common among all classes. The slave trade flourished with its violence and disregard for human worth. Smuggling and gambling were constant problems and thievery was rampant. Immorality was common. The lot of the working people was almost unbearable. The suffering of poverty-stricken families intensified because breadwinners were imprisoned for debts. A laborer's life was one of drudgery under miserable working conditions. Young children slaved in mines and mills for up to 14 hours a day.

The religious life of England was not any better. Sermons in the churches had become little more than dry and colorless talks on morality. Most of the clergy seemed to care little for their congregations, being more interested in fox hunting, card playing, and drinking.

Into this society John and Charles Wesley were born to Samuel and Susannah Wesley. Both Charles and John attended Christ Church College in Oxford and in 1729 John was ordained to the ministry.

When Samuel Wesley died in 1735, John would have been pleased to become the pastor in Epworth where his father had ministered, but a call for young men to do missionary work in the newly established American colony of Georgia captured both him and Charles. Their mother urged them to go, saying, "Had I 20 sons I would rejoice that they were all so employed, though I should never see them any more" (B. K. Kuiper, *The Church in History*, Eerdmans, p. 286).

John and Charles labored hard in Georgia, but were ineffective. Charles became ill and returned to England within a year of his arrival in America. Two years later, John returned. The Wesleys had failed because they lacked the most important ingredient necessary for success as missionaries: genuine conversion to Christ. Shortly that would change.

On May 21, 1738 Charles came to genuine faith in Christ. Three days later, John was converted at a meeting of an Anglican society on Aldersgate Street. Of this experience, John later wrote: "About a quarter before nine, while I was listening to Luther's description of the change which God works in the heart through faith in Christ, I felt my heart strangely warmed. I felt I did trust in Christ, Christ alone for salvation; and an assurance was given me, that He had taken away my sins, even mine, and saved me from the law of sin and death" (Kuiper, *The Church*, p. 287).

The Wesleys' new message of conversion closed most of the pulpits of the established church to John and Charles, but spiritually-starved England needed their message and God broke down barriers and opened doors to allow their voices to be heard. B. K. Kuiper also relates, "It was in this England, growing in wealth and power but religiously stagnant and morally corrupt—an England lighted by only a few stray and feeble gleams—that John Wesley, with the help of his brother Charles and their friend George Whitefield, began his mighty work" (*The Church*, p. 289).

Since the churches were closed to them, American evangelist George Whitefield invited the Wesleys to join him in preaching in the open fields. John hesitated at first—preaching anywhere but in a church was a great hurdle for this properly trained minister; however he could not resist meeting needy coal miners and others where they lived. The opening of John's heart to the needs of the poor was a key factor in the Wesleys bringing revival to England.

Like all great spiritual awakenings, the Wesleyan Revival was born in prayer. Whole nights were spent in intercessory prayer. At length God answered. In *When the Fire Fell*, George T. B. Davis writes: "Filled with the Spirit of God, Wesley and Whitefield and others went everywhere preaching the Gospel. Like a gale from heaven they went up and down the British Isles preaching to vast multitudes sometimes numbering 20,000 and more" (The Million Testaments Campaigns, p. 17).

The Wesleyan Revival transformed England. In its wake millions were born again, the Sunday School movement was started, the slave trade ended, prison reforms were instituted, humane labor laws were passed, and the general moral climate of the nation was greatly improved. Kuiper says: "The England Wesley left behind him was so different from the England he found that it was almost unrecognizable. He had transformed it" (*The Church*, p. 295).

Born out of the Wesleyan Revival were Charles Wesley's hymns. The music composed during that time of refreshing carries some of the Wesleyan Revival to churches around the world week after week today.

Reasons for the success of the Wesleyan ministries seem to be a strong emphasis on prayer, straightforward preaching of the Gospel, a consuming passion for souls, the willingness to minister to neglected people, and John Wesley's ability to organize believers into groups to nourish converts and build up all believers.

The Revival of 1858

The Revival of 1858 has been called America's greatest. Certainly the need for revival was great in the mid-19th century. Violence and immorality were widespread. Churches were torn with strife and cults were multiplying.

In his book, *Will Revival Come?* Earnest M. Wadsworth says of that era:

The nation was generally prosperous. Railroads and water transportation expanded trade. New towns and cities sprang up everywhere. National and international trade greatly increased. . . . English and American authors were enjoying great popularity. Infidelity and atheism were rampant. The writings of Tom Paine and of European infidels were read by multitudes. Prosperity gave the people much leisure for reading and discussion. Multitudes turned from the churches and busied themselves in politics, education, and amusements. The consciences of men became hardened. Indifference to spiritual religion generally prevailed (Moody Press, p. 13).

The revival, which began in New York City, seems to have originated in the prayer life of one Jeremiah Lanphier. Many others undoubtedly contributed to this historic awakening, but Lanphier arranged the prayer meetings in which the revival was born.

He was a quiet and zealous businessman who accepted an appointment to be a city missionary for the North Dutch Reformed Church in Lower Manhattan. His task was difficult. He often became discouraged, but drew strength from prayer to go on. Believing that others might find help for their needs by joining him in prayer, he announced a series of weekly noon-hour prayer meetings, the first of which was to be held September 23, 1857. The printed announcements of the prayer meetings explained that they were to last for an hour, but were designed also for those who found it inconvenient to remain more than 5 or 10 minutes.

In the first meeting, Lanphier prayed alone for the first half hour. Then others came till a total of six were praying. The next week the number increased and by the first week of October, it was decided to hold the prayer meetings daily instead of weekly.

In October there were two important events that helped

move the people of North America to revival. In the first week, coinciding with the daily prayer meetings in New York City, revival broke out in Hamilton, Ontario where Walter and Phoebe Palmer, a physician and his talented wife, were holding meetings. During the second week of October a financial panic set in that prostrated business everywhere. Of these three developments J. Edwin Orr has written in *The Fervent Prayer*:

It is impossible not to connect the three events, for in them was demonstrated the need of religious revival, the means by which to accomplish it, and the provision of divine grace to meet the serious situation in church and society.

From tiny springs of prayer in New York and preaching in Hamilton came a flood soon to envelop the world. The United States received the blessing first, then the United Kingdom, Australia, South Africa, and South India.

Within six months, 10 thousand businessmen were gathering daily for prayer in New York. Within two years, 1 million converts were added to the American churches. No part of the nation remained untouched by fervent prayer (Moody Press, pp. 4-5).

The revival that reached full bloom in 1858 caused churches to spread across the frontier and flourish in the cities. The moral fiber of the nation was strengthened. Missionary work expanded at home and abroad. Out of this revival grew the great evangelistic ministry of D. L. Moody with its far-reaching effects.

Conclusion

Today's evangelistic efforts in local churches, area-wide evangelistic crusades, and the ministries of media preachers are the results of patterns and practices developed in the great historical revivals. Local revivals and those that are larger in scope are blessed but fall far short of the mighty movings of God in the past.

While we should be grateful for the great revivals and their effects on us, we cannot survive on past blessings. We need another great spiritual awakening. No generation has faced a crisis more serious than the one in which we find ourselves today.

Where is the Jonathan Edwards, the John Wesley, or the Jeremiah Lanphier for this crucial hour? What man or woman among us will lead the church to its knees? Will the "times of refreshing" ever come again?

10 CAN WE HAVE REVIVAL NOW?

Revival is the key to survival.

Survival may mean complete deliverance from danger by divine intervention as Nineveh was spared. It may be the delivering of England from bloody revolution because of the transformation and reforms brought about by the Wesleyan Revival.

Survival may also mean God's preservation in extreme difficulties as was the case with the early church. Triumph in a time of suffering was also the lot of believers during the American Civil War. That conflict could not put out the fire that had started in Jeremiah Lanphier's prayer meeting, and great numbers of people came to Christ in spite of the tears and terrors of the war between the states.

Prerequisite to Revival: Extreme Need

Many people know 2 Chronicles 7:19, the most used revival text: "If My people, which are called by My name, shall humble themselves, and pray, and seek My face, and turn from their wicked ways; then will I hear from heaven, and will forgive their sin, and will heal their land." But few know 2 Chronicles 7:13: "If I shut up heaven that there be no rain, or if I command the locusts to devour the land, or if I send pestilence among My people."

Revivals generally come about during times of extreme need. In Israel's case, the neglect of God's Word and disobedience to His precepts produced conditions designed to call the people to revival. God's promise guaranteed forgiveness and the healing of the land upon the humble, prayerful, earnest, and righteous response of the people.

God has not changed.

Some feel the church is past reviving and the nation past changing. They see a slumbering, self-satisfied church in a society immersed in greed, lust, crime, and unbelief. They hopelessly throw up their hands in despair. There is no question that social and moral conditions are grievous and the church is in need, but this combination has never placed revival beyond the reach of those who desired it.

Dr. John R. Rice has written:

All through recorded history one truth stands out forever the same. God has given revivals in spite of man's wickedness, in spite of man's unworthiness, his unbelief, and unfaithfulness. . . . God must feel it as an insult to His power and grace that people think revivals can only be had in propitious circumstances. . . . What sin, what reproach upon God, what a mark of our unbelief, when we indicate that conditions are too hard for God, that conditions prevent a revival. History down through all the ages cries that it is a lie! All the revivals in Bible times, the great Reformation revival with Luther and Calvin and others, the Wesleyan revival that saved England from its French Revolution and made English and American civilization and freedom what is today, the Moody revivals and more— these were all brought about in the face of horrible, widespread, and flagrant sin, in the face of spiritual decline and unbelief in the churches and out (*We Can Have Revival Now*, Sword of the Lord, pp. 129, 133, 134-135).

The fact that revivals come in difficult times should encourage us to pray for revival and expect it. This was the attitude of the psalmist: "Wilt thou not revive us again: that thy people may rejoice in thee" (Ps. 85:6).

There are two ways in which to look at the history of revivals in the church: We may glory in them, but conclude that the days of great revivals are forever past or we may, like the psalmist, rejoice that the God who has repeatedly revived His people in their times of need can do it again.

Is Revival Possible Today?

Some earnest believers rule out revival in our time because they think such an event would be contrary to God's prophetic plan. Observing the movements of nations on the world stage, the knowledge explosion, and other end-time signs, they conclude that revival is not on the program. They point to Scripture references that describe increased wickedness in the last days: "'And many false prophets shall rise, and shall deceive many. And because iniquity shall abound, the love of many shall wax cold" (Matt. 24:11-12). "Now the Spirit speaketh expressly, that in the latter times some shall depart from the faith, giving heed to seducing spirits, and doctrines of devils; speaking lies in hypocrisy; having their conscience seared with a hot iron" (1 Tim. 4:1-2). "Knowing this first, that there shall come in the last days scoffers, walking after their own lusts, and saying, 'Where is the promise of His coming? For since the fathers fell asleep, all things continue as they were from the beginning of creation'" (2 Peter 3:3-4).

Notice that none of these texts rule out revival. The conditions prophesied will and do exist, but such conditions were present before and after America's greatest revival. Even a revival of momentous proportions does not root out all the evil in a nation. There are still millions of people unconverted and in deep sin.

Another factor must be considered: We do not know the year of our Lord's return (Matt. 24:36). To say that revival cannot come because we are too near to the return of Christ is to say more than we know.

A belief that we are fast approaching the fulfillment of Christ's promise to return should call any believer to revival. If we are living in the closing moments of the age, now is the time to surrender ourselves totally to the Holy Spirit, giving Him every area of our lives. John encouraged his readers to "abide in Him; that, when He shall appear, we may have confidence, and not be ashamed before Him at His coming" (1 John 2:28). We should be motivated to personal revival and holy living, as John said, "Beloved, now are we the sons of God, and it doth not yet appear what we shall be: but we know that, when He shall appear, we shall be like Him; for we shall see Him as He is. And every man that hath this hope in Him purifieth himself, even as He is pure" (1 John 3:2-3).

People who genuinely believe in Christ's imminent coming will be the first to seek revival. It is one thing to talk prophecy and quite another to allow end-time truths to change our lives. Whatever the world conditions in the last days, Christians need to clean their spiritual houses, return to their first love, and do personal evangelism. This translates into revival.

We can have revival now because God's power is not diminished. He is still able to refresh His people. In the Great Commission, He promised to provide power for believers for all time. "And Jesus came and spake unto them, saying, 'All power is given unto Me in heaven and in earth.

Go ye therefore, and teach all nations, baptizing them in the name of the Father, and of the Son, and of the Holy Ghost: teaching them to observe all things whatsoever I have commanded you: and, lo, I am with you alway, even unto the end of the world. Amen' " (Matt. 28:18-20).

The empowering Holy Spirit who came at Pentecost remains today. He indwells each believer just as He has done through the centuries. A well-meaning Christian, moved by the wickedness of the times and the seeming inability of churches to stem the tide of sin, said he thought the Holy Spirit was being gradually removed from the world in the last days. He was wrong. Believers are still here; their bodies are still temples of the Holy Spirit, as Paul said, "What? know ye not that your body is the temple of the Holy Ghost which is in you, which ye have of God, and ye are not your own? For ye are bought with a price: therefore glorify God in your body, and in your spirit which are God's" (1 Cor. 6:19-20). The command for all believers to be filled with the Holy Spirit is still in force: "And be not drunk with wine, wherein is excess, but be filled with the Spirit" (Eph. 5:18).

When Revival Comes

A Spirit-filled Christian is a revived Christian. And when the members of a local church are filled with the Holy Spirit, revival has come to the church. Imagine your church reflecting Ephesians 5:19-21: "Speaking to yourselves in psalms and hymns and spiritual songs, singing and making melody in your heart to the Lord; giving thanks always for all things unto God and the Father in the name of our Lord Jesus Christ; submitting yourselves one to another in the fear of God."

Think of all the barriers between believers in your local fellowship broken down; all wrongs made right. Imagine all the malice put away and the gossiping ceased. Picture the impact on your community if the fruit of the Spirit (Gal. 5:22-23) was evident in every church member's life. Consider the growth explosion that would take place in your church if every member cared for the lost as did Spirit-filled Paul.

What if God should want to begin a nation-changing revival in your church? Would you be in favor of that? Do you think it is possible? Or have you relegated all of God's greatest blessings to the past?

Do you think your church is the most unlikely place on earth for God to do a mighty work? Then take heart. Revivals begin in the most unlikely places. Dr. John R. Rice aptly said:

If God could give a revival in Jerusalem at Pentecost, He can give one anywhere. Never a city, never a country in the world where people have hated Christ more than they hated Him at Jerusalem. Never a city or country in the world where they have rejected more pure Gospel, and have despised more the manifestation of God's grace, than at Jerusalem. Nowhere in the world is there a place where God's disciples have failed Him so signally as that little band of disciples seemed to have failed Christ in the hours of His arrest, trial, and death. They did not even believe that He had risen from the dead. They had thrown away all their hopes. Peter had quit the ministry and had gone back to fishing. Thomas would not believe in His resurrection for a week after others had been convinced of it. But the Lord Jesus met and empowered those disciples and used them in a mighty, mighty revival!

We know God can give us a revival now because He gave one in Jerusalem, at Pentecost. How foolish to suppose that times are getting too hard for God, or hearts are getting too hard for God, or circumstances are too difficult for God to deal with! Oh, rather how we ought to say that our great God, with the power of the Word of God and the power of the Spirit of God and in answer to the prayers of His believing people, can give a revival anywhere, when we meet His requirements and pay His price! (*We Can*, pp. 92-93)

Can we have revival now? Absolutely.

God is ready. Are we?

11 WHERE REVIVAL BEGINS

A danger in focusing on great revivals is that we may think of them only in full flame and forget their humble beginnings.

All great revivals began in a small way.

Evangelist Gypsy Smith was once asked how to start a revival. He replied, "Go home, lock yourself in your room, and kneel down in the middle of your floor. Draw a chalk mark all around yourself and ask God to start the revival inside that chalk mark. When He has answered your prayer, the revival will be on" (Walter B. Knight, *Knight's Master Book of New Illustrations*, Eerdmans, p. 568).

Human Responsibility
In his book *Flames of Freedom*, Erwin W. Lutzer says that many people think revival is much like lightning except you can consider yourself fortunate if you are struck by it (Moody Press, p. 137). This "struck by lightning" view, however, does not hold up under careful study of either the Scriptures or the great revivals of history. The guarantee of 2 Chroni-

cles 7:14 calls for human response to God's invitation to blessing. Even if this promise is only for Israel, one cannot discount the prayers and surrender of believers involved in the birth of past revivals.

In recounting the story of the 1949 revival in the Hebrides, Duncan Campbell says:

I personally believe in the sovereignty of God in the affairs of men, but I do not believe in any concept of service that eliminates man's responsibility. Here are men and women who believe in a covenant-keeping God; who believe that the God to whom they pray could not fail to keep His covenanted engagements; but they also believe that they too had something to do about it. God was the God of revival, but they were the instruments, the agents through which revival was possible. I heard one of the elders of the church praying: "Lord, You must do it, for we cannot; but we want to tell You now that we are here before You as empty vessels for You to fill" (quoted in *Heart Cry for Revival*, Revell, p. 28).

R. A. Torrey's prescription for revival also involved human responsibility. He wrote:

First, let a few Christians (they need not be many) get thoroughly right with God themselves. This is the prime essential. If this is not done, the rest that I am to say will come to nothing.

Second, let them bind themselves together in a prayer group to pray for revival till God opens the heavens and comes down.

Third, let them put themselves at the disposal of God for Him to use as He sees fit in winning others to Christ.

That is all!

This is sure to bring a revival to any church or community. I have given this prescription around the world. It has been taken by many churches and many communities, and in no instance has it ever failed; and it cannot fail (Knight, *Master Book*, p. 568).

Torrey's prescription seems to touch all the bases. It contains five essentials in bringing a genuine spiritual awakening: concern, conviction, prayer, surrender, and love. When the human instruments respond to these needs, revival, at least to some degree, is sure to come.

Concern

Every heaven-sent revival begins with some person's burning concern about moral decline and spiritual apathy in the community and the church.

The Prophet Isaiah expressed God's feelings about so few being concerned.

For our transgressions are multiplied before Thee, and our sins testify against us: for our transgressions are with us; and as for our iniquities, we know them; in transgressing and lying against the Lord, and departing away from our God, speaking oppression and revolt, conceiving and uttering from the heart words of falsehood. And judgment is turned away backward, and justice standeth afar off:

For truth is fallen in the street, and equity cannot enter. Yea truth faileth; and he that departeth from evil maketh himself a prey: and the Lord saw it, and it displeased Him that there was no judgment. *And He saw that there was no man, and wondered that there was no intercessor* (Isa. 59:12-16; italics added).

Today there are so many things that move the sensitive heart. Moral conditions of our time are similar to those of England before the Wesleyan revival. Spiritual life is lacking. Foreign enemies stand poised to destroy us. If there ever was a generation born to legitimate concern, ours is the one. But is concern enough?

Conviction

It is one thing to be concerned about the sins of the community and quite another to be convicted of personal sins. Many are grieved over national shortcomings but have not taken the time to inspect their own lives. Some willingly demonstrate against certain sins of the nation but are not nearly so judgmental about their own sins.

Isaiah the prophet lived in a time like ours—moral decay and spiritual apathy were rampant—and he spoke out against these sins. He pronounced a number of woes upon his people—and then experienced deep personal conviction. He cried, "Woe is me! for I am undone; because I am a man of unclean lips, and I dwell in the midst of a people of unclean lips: for mine eyes have seen the King, the Lord of hosts" (Isa. 6:5).

No wonder his life was changed.

Revival always begins with one or more believers getting thoroughly right with God. The great evangelist Charles Finney said, "Since a revival can never lay hold upon the world until it first lays hold on the church, the need is for the fountains of sin to be broken up in the church. Backslidden Christians must be brought to repentance. They must have their faith renewed. Before the world can be moved, we must renew the image of Jesus Christ in ourselves" (Walter B. Knight, *Knight's Treasury of Illustrations*, Eerdmans, p. 322).

While seeking revival in the Hebrides, a group of Christians prayed together in a barn three nights a week for months. Finally, after reading from Psalm 24, one young man closed his Bible and said, "Brethren, it is just so much humbug to be waiting thus night after night, month after month, if we ourselves are not right with God. I must ask myself—'Is my heart pure? Are my hands clean?' " Conviction had broken through. Only then did the long awaited revival come (Olford, *Heart Cry*, pp. 28-29).

Unless we are willing to face our sins, we can talk about revival, study the techniques of revival, and even pray for revival, all to no avail. Sins we tolerate must be confessed and forsaken; then personal revival will come.

Prayer

D. L. Moody observed that every great work of God can be traced to a kneeling figure.

It has always been so.

The early church prayed and revival came.

Jonathan Edwards prayed, issued a call to prayer, and revival came.

The Wesleys prayed long into the night with a company of Christians longing for spiritual awakening in England, and revival came.

Jeremiah Lanphier started his noonday prayer meetings, and revival came.

Where are the prayer-warriors of our day who will not rest till revival comes?

Stressing prayer as a requisite of revival, Charles Finney said: "Prayer is an essential link in the chain of causes that leads to a revival; as much so as truth is. Some have zealously used truth to convert men, and laid very little stress on prayer. They have preached, and talked, and distributed tracts with great zeal, and then wondered that they had so little success. And the reason was, that they forgot to use the other branch of the means, effectual prayer" (*Revivals of Religion*, Moody Press, pp. 48-49). Leonard Ravenhill has written: "Poverty-stricken as the church is today in many things, she is most stricken here, in the place of prayer. . . . Failing here, we fail everywhere" (*Why Revival Tarries*, Bethany Fellowship, p. 7).

But we do not have to fail!

Invitations to pray and receive abound in Scripture. Only a few can be quoted here. God's message through Jeremiah was: "Call unto Me, and I will answer thee and show thee great and mighty things, which thou knowest not" (Jer. 33:3). Jesus said, "Ask, and it shall be given you; seek, and ye shall find; knock, and it shall be opened unto you: for every one that asketh receiveth; and he that seeketh findeth; and to him that knocketh it shall be opened" (Matt. 7:7-8).

The list goes on.

Do you long for personal revival? Pray for it. Do you want a revival in your church? Start a prayer group. Seize every opportunity to move fellowship gatherings to prayer. Have church board meetings where the entire business time is given to prayer. Call special congregational meetings just to pray for revival. And the God of revival will hear your prayers.

Do you desire revival throughout the nation? Pray big. Expect God to begin a work in you and in your church that cannot be contained in one congregation. A great awakening may await your prayers.

Surrender

The four most difficult words to pray are these: "Thy will be done." They express total surrender, the sacrifice of self for the glory of God. But total surrender is necessary if revival is to come.

The hymn of surrender, "Have Thine Own Way, Lord!" may be the clearest extrabiblical expression of revival truth to be found. Read it alone and in groups without the music. Sing it often on your knees. Let its message sink deeply into your heart. Make it the theme of your life.

Personal revival is letting God have His way in our lives. When an entire church chooses God's will over individual desire, a church-wide revival is taking place. When cheerful surrender to the will of God becomes the experience of believers across an entire state or nation, the times of refreshing have arrived.

Love

My work as a consultant on revival and church growth and as a speaker on revival and prophecy takes me to churches of all spiritual temperatures. Sometimes I have the delightful task of recognizing a revival already in progress and calling the attention of the congregation to what is happening among them.

Recently a family thanked me for letting them know a revival was going on. They had been praying for revival in their church, but the idea that revival only sweeps across an entire nation had blinded them to the fact of the genuine spiritual awakening taking place in their own congregation.

This family's church had gone through a period of serious decline. Attendance had dropped 75 percent; strife had torn the church apart. Eight pastors had served the church in a 5-year period. The future seemed bleak in spite of the fine facilities that had been constructed during better times.

Then came a pastor who loved the people of the church and cared for lost souls. By the time I arrived for a conference on revival and prophecy he had been serving there for 11 months. Attendance had tripled. Barriers between believers had been broken down. Conversions were taking place regularly. The joy of the Lord was evident among the people. Revival had come.

Another church was near closing. Attendance was small and interest waning. One board member and his family, often the only ones at the midweek service, sometimes wondered if it might be well to remain at home and pray. But they continued meeting at church to let the neighborhood know there was a service there on Wednesday night.

The man who accepted this unpromising pastorate believed the congregation and the population in the surrounding area would respond to love. This was his first church, but his confidence in God's love and power was unshakable. Within eight months the church building was packed on Sunday mornings. When I came for a conference on revival and prophecy, it was clear that I had arrived too late to help start a revival. The revival was well under way and the members of the church knew it.

That the key to revival in both of these churches was love is not surprising when one remembers Paul's warning that the most eloquent teaching and preaching without love is just noise (1 Cor. 13:1-3). Yet many churches hope to have revival without meeting the need for love.

Christians determined to cling to malice and bitterness should not expect revival. Those who are unwilling to forgive others should not look for a spiritual awakening. Believers who will not allow the Lord to move them to see a lost world through eyes of love must not hope for times of refreshing. Laying aside hindrances to love will open the door to revival in these times.

Conclusion

We live on the brink. Our survival may depend on our spiritual temperature. The fate of the nation may rest in our hands. There is gain in being in the place of blessing. Let us flee there. Draw that circle and let revival begin in you. Who knows how far the holy flame will spread?

12 THE SAFE RETREAT

Twenty years ago, when the Civil Defense Department promoted the construction of home bomb shelters, the idea sounded so good that I ordered instruction booklets and placed them on a table in the foyer of the church I was pastoring.

One of the most spiritual men of the church stood near the literature table eyeing the stack of lifesavers.

"I don't think we'll need them," he said.

"Why not?" I asked.

"I believe the Lord will take care of us," he replied.

My friend and Christian brother who scorned the bomb shelter booklets is now in heaven. He never needed a bomb shelter. He already had one. He was absolutely sure that God would care for him in life and receive him to heaven when the journey was over.

The Sheltered Life

The psalmist spoke often of the God-sheltered life. In these Psalms the theme of God's protection is a recurring one:

Thou art my hiding place; Thou shalt preserve me from trouble; Thou shalt compass me about with songs of deliverance (32:7).

God is our refuge and strength, a very present help in trouble. Therefore will not we fear, though the earth be removed, and though the mountains be carried into the midst of the sea; though the waters thereof roar and be troubled, though the mountains shake with the swelling thereof (46:1-3).

Thou are my hiding place and my shield: I hope in Thy Word (119:114).

These passages do not imply that it is wrong for Christians to prepare against a day of trouble or that seeking shelter when the bombs are falling demonstrates a lack of faith. The early Christians survived for a time by hiding in the catacombs, though they didn't build them. They were too busy evangelizing to prepare earthly fortresses in which to wait out the Roman persecution, but when they needed a place to hide, God provided one.

We have wandered far from first-century Christianity. "Strangers and pilgrims" they were called (1 Peter 2:11). As citizens of heaven, they thought of themselves as just passing through (Phil. 3:20). We have put our roots down deep. No wonder it is so difficult to keep our priorities right—we have so many holdings on this planet that we can't bear to think of leaving them.

Still, like it or not, our stay here is limited. We are transients. Medical science can lengthen life, modern weaponry can shorten it, but one thing is certain: a Christian who is in the center of God's will is safe till his task on earth is complete. Then he will be taken home. That's two-way security.

This assurance was characteristic of New Testament Christianity. Consider Paul's dilemma: "For to me to live is Christ, and to die is gain. But if I live in the flesh, this is the fruit of my labour: yet what I shall choose I want not. For I am in a strait betwixt two, having a desire to depart and be with Christ; which is far better" (Phil. 1:21-23).

People on the brink have no guarantees. Hideaways built in supposedly safe zones may prove to be death traps. Money hidden away may be stolen or become worthless. Trusted political candidates may betray their supporters. Weapons intended to protect may lead to an accidental war. Peace treaties which seem secure may turn out to be negotiated destruction. Paul warned, "When they shall say, 'Peace and safety'; then sudden destruction cometh upon them, as travail upon a woman with child; and they shall not escape" (1 Thes. 5:3).

The Way to Survival
The center of God's will is the safest place on earth to be, because our Lord cares for His own. The Prophet Nahum said, "The Lord is good, a stronghold in the day of trouble; and He knoweth them that trust in Him" (1:7). In Proverbs we read, "The name of the Lord is a strong tower: the righteous runneth into it, and is safe" (18:10).

Have you trusted in Christ as your Lord and Saviour?

Have you fully surrendered to Him?

Then rest in His care. Get busy about your Lord's business, taking His Gospel to others in both life and word while there is time. Don't waste time cowering. You live in the circle of His love.

In the Circle of His Love
Nothing can befall you apart from God's will. Paul wrote, "And we know that all things work together for good to them that love God, to them who are the called according to His purpose" (Rom. 8:28).

Understanding that God was able to protect him, David wrote, "My times are in Thy hand" (Ps. 31:15). Perhaps one of heaven's surprises will be finding out how many times God has spared our lives.

Elisha once appeared to be in great danger. The King of Syria had sent a large military force to destroy the prophet. Elisha's servant, seeing the great army coming, was paralyzed with fear. But Elisha was calm, telling him not to be afraid because there were more standing around them than were pursuing them. The servant was confused. Then "Elisha prayed, and said, 'Lord, I pray Thee, open his eyes, that he may see.' And the Lord opened the eyes of the young man; and he saw: and behold, the mountain was full of horses and chariots of fire round about Elisha" (2 Kings 6:17).

Scheming Babylonian politicians could not destroy Daniel in the lion's den nor his three friends in the fiery furnace because God protected them.

The God who protected His people in Bible times is our God today. When John Wesley was six years old, his father's house went up in flames. All the children were taken to safety except John, who was forgotten till someone heard him crying. His father ran to the stairs, but they were so nearly consumed with flames they would not bear his weight. In despair he fell on his knees and asked God for help.

In the meantime, young John had climbed up on a chest. The neighbors standing by saw him and quickly rescued him by hoisting one man on the shoulders of another. A moment later the roof fell in.

Godly Samuel Wesley cried out, "Come, neighbors, let us kneel down; let us give thanks to God. He has given me all my children. Let the house go, I am rich enough."

The incident so impressed John Wesley that under one of his portraits he wrote, "Is not this a brand plucked out of the

burning?" (Walter B. Knight, *Knight's Master Book of New Illustrations*, Eerdmans, p. 532)

John Wesley could not be lost to the fire. God's purpose in his life must be fulfilled.

During the Reformation a man tried to frighten Martin Luther by telling him that in a crisis he would lose all of his support.

"And where will you be then?" the foe taunted.

Luther's reply was simple. "Where I am now," he said, "In the hands of Almighty God" (Knight, *Master Book*, p. 527).

Conclusion

Certainly there are many things to trouble us in this dangerous period of history. But our God is greater than all of our perils. The world is in trouble, but God's program is being carried out. Nothing takes Him by surprise. We cannot escape the news of anxiety-producing events but we can trust our Lord to deliver us in spite of them.

Of one thing we may be sure, we can never escape the external stimuli that cause vexation. The world is full of them and though we were to retreat to a cave and live the remainder of our days alone we still could not lose them. The rough floor of our cave would chafe us, the weather would irritate us and the very silence would cause us to fret.

Let us look out calmly upon the world; or better yet, let us look down upon it from above where Christ is seated and we are seated in Him (A. W. Tozer, *Man, The Dwelling Place of God*, Christian Publications, p. 69).

As storm clouds gather overhead, there is a place to hide. Isaiah said prophetically of Jesus: "A man shall be as an hiding place from the wind, and a covert from the tempest; as rivers of water in a dry place, as the shadow of a great rock in a weary land" (Isa. 32:2).

Come, lay aside your fears and hide in Him.